DISASTERS *of* ONTARIO

75 Stories of Courage & Chaos

René Biberstein

FOLK
LORE
PUBLISHING

© 2007 by Folklore Publishing
First printed in 2007 10 9 8 7 6 5 4 3 2 1
Printed in Canada

The Publisher: Folklore Publishing
Website: www.folklorepublishing.com

Library and Archives Canada Cataloguing in Publication

Biberstein, René
    Disaster's of Ontario : 75 stories of courage & chaos / by René Biberstein.

ISBN 13: 978-1-894864-14-5
ISBN 10: 1-894864-14-X

    1. Disaster's of Ontario

Project Director: Faye Boer
Project Editor: Kathy van Denderen
Production: Michael Cooke, Trina Koscielnuk
Photo Credits: Every effort has been made to accurately credit the sources of photographs. Any errors or omissions should be reported directly to the publisher for correction in future editions. Photographs courtesy of Archives of Ontario (p. 130, C281-0-0-0-34; p. 165, C7-4-0-0-44, John Boyd fonds); Library and Archives Canada (p. 41, S.J. Dixon/PA-120552; p. 46, PA-028750; p. 53, Henry Peters/PA-029808); Maritime History of the Great Lakes (p. 183); Michigan Maritime Museum Collection (p. 93); Mississauga Library System (p. 217, M466); Niagara Falls Public Library (p. 80, D11282R); Toronto Archives (p. 10, 115, 157, 243, Series 402, Item 8); Toronto Region and Conservation (p. 89); Steven Van Seggelen (p. 237).

We acknowledge the financial support of the Alberta Foundation for the Arts for our publishing program.

We acknowledge the financial support of the Government of Canada through the Book Publishing Industry Development Program for our publishing activities.

Alberta Foundation for the Arts

Canada Council for the Arts   Conseil des Arts du Canada   Canadian Heritage   Patrimoine canadien

PC:P5

Dedication

Who built the seven gates of Thebes?
The books are filled with names of kings.
Was it the kings who hauled the craggy blocks of stone?...
Each page a victory
At whose expense the victory ball?

—Berthold Brecht

THIS BOOK IS DEDICATED TO ALL THOSE WHO HAVE DIED IN Ontario's disasters, natural and accidental, and those who may die in disasters of the future. When we consider what we have today, we should think of them.

Acknowledgement

ONCE AGAIN, SPECIAL ACKNOWLEDGEMENT GOES TO Laurel Christie for her help on the book. She was able to provide me with most of the research for *Disasters of Ontario*. Laurel is equally responsible for this book's existence.

Table of Contents

III—Wartime Disasters

Introduction

＊

ONTARIO'S HISTORY HAS BEEN A LONG ROAD filled with dramatic twists—but not all those twists have been pleasant. When we picture the province's past, we tend to think of railways, canals and cities being built, or of great politicians or generals. We often forget that for all the success achieved, there were trains that crashed, ships that sunk, cities that burned, and politicians and military men who made disastrous decisions.

This book, *Disasters of Ontario*, is about those tragedies. It is also, in particular, about the victims of tragedy. Most of them were ordinary people who perished while doing what they usually did—travelling, sailing, mining, fighting fires or even relaxing at home. These people, who were much like most of us—regular folks—rarely get talked about. Their names and stories are quickly forgotten. One of the unfortunate—though largely unavoidable— elements of history is that we remember only a few famous faces from the past.

Sometimes it takes a disaster to bring these ordinary people to our attention. But how exactly do you define a disaster? After all, there are disasters of all scales, from small, personal crises to epidemics that killed tens of thousands. And people describe dinner parties as "disastrous," for that matter.

In my view, a disaster is a shocking and unexpected event that causes—or threatens to cause—a major loss of lives. It can be natural, accidental or deliberate. Nonfatal disasters, such as the Mississauga train derailment, are included in the book because they threatened much deadlier results. I have also included ongoing problems that quietly killed thousands, such as the polio epidemic, and the diseases that wiped out much of Ontario's Aboriginal population when Europeans first arrived.

Deadly periods in war are not part of this account, such as the battles in the War of 1812, because soldiers' deaths are hardly surprising in times of war. I have also excluded disasters that affected Ontarians travelling or living outside of Ontario, such the Air India bombings and the September 11 hijackings.

Ontario's disasters have been all over the map—literally and figuratively. But above all else, the province is notorious for its brutal and sudden lake squalls. Those who haven't experienced the Great Lakes might well wonder how so many people could have drowned in such small, comparatively shallow bodies of water, often within sight of the shore. Indeed, there is not a single area of comparative size in any ocean that has caused so many shipwrecks.

A few factors might help to explain this. The fresh water of the Great Lakes is less buoyant than the salt water of oceans, leading ships—and people—to sink more easily. The lakes are also infamous for their storms, particularly in November, when heavy rain comes up the Mississippi Valley from the Gulf of Mexico and collides with freezing Arctic winds coming down from the Hudson Bay. In addition, the narrow rocky passages that ships must often navigate their way through necessitates that Great Lakes ships be smaller than ocean-going ships, leaving them more vulnerable to high winds and waves. And finally— as with all dangerous places for ships worldwide—the Great Lakes have their share of curses, supernatural tales and "hoodoos."

Chief among these curses is the notion—of questionable accuracy—of the Marysburgh Vortex, an area of eastern Lake Ontario and the western St. Lawrence River where ships are said to disappear into without a trace.

Although improved communication and navigation technology has dramatically reduced the number of shipping disasters on the lakes since the late 19th century, it hasn't been able to completely tame the five bodies of water. Disasters can still happen, as the crew of the *Edmund Fitzgerald* fatefully discovered in 1975.

Fires have also devastated the lives of Ontarians. Northern Ontario—like all parts of northern Canada—suffers from regular summer forest fires, often spreading to a size and intensity that boggles the imagination. During the first period of major settlement in the north in the early 20th century, some of these fires had exceptionally fatal results. Mining boom towns that had sprung up overnight—like Matheson or South Porcupine—virtually disappeared in a single day, along with many of their citizens.

We often forget today that cities used to be regularly destroyed by fire. Poor firefighting technology, a proliferation of wood and coal stoves, and lack of building codes all contributed to many urban fires. Nearly all of Ontario's major cities—Toronto, Ottawa, Kingston and London—have been incinerated in fire at some point (or several points, in some cases). The casualties of these fires came from the bottom to the top of society—even the Parliament buildings in Ottawa burned to the ground in 1916. (Take note that in this book, "firemen" are distinguished from "firefighters." Those who tended the engines of steam locomotives by filling them with coal and water were historically known as "firemen.")

There have also been many railway disasters. Although rail travel is regarded as consistently safer than road travel, when accidents do occur, they can be monumental. The province's worst railway disasters occurred in the early years of this form of transport, when schedules and construction standards were only loosely adhered to. The tragic results are probably best illustrated in the Desjardins Canal railway bridge collapse, which caused an entire passenger train to plunge into the icy waters below.

Disasters of weather, such as Hurricane Hazel, surprised a complacent population who thought that hurricanes could not reach so far inland. There have been tornadoes—so many of them in fact, that a part of south-western Ontario has been nicknamed "Tornado Alley." Most of the tornadoes had little serious effect, but some were disastrous to property and lives. The Ice Storm of 1998, which froze most of eastern Ontario along with Québec, left many people without water or power, or a way out, for over a month.

And finally, epidemics have wreaked more havoc than any other form of disaster in Ontario—albeit at a slower, less dramatic pace. Typhus, cholera, the Spanish Influenza and polio all rolled across Ontario as they did the rest of North America. More recently—though on a much smaller scale—the SARS crisis struck Toronto with a focused ferocity.

This book doesn't aim to be an organized "top ten list" of the worst disasters in the province's history. Rather, it tries to bring together a wide range of tragedies, from all corners of Ontario and from many different categories, explaining their details and telling the stories of the people involved.

It is my hope that you will be enlightened by it and will remember the victims of Ontario's tragedies of the past and present.

Part I
Natural Disasters

Sinking of the *Ontario*

—————— ✦ ——————

October 31–November 1, 1780
Lake Ontario

LITTLE IS KNOWN ABOUT one of the worst early shipping disasters in the Great Lakes: the loss of the British warship *Ontario*.

In 1780, the *Ontario* was only one year old. The American Revolutionary War was still technically underway, though it had been all but lost by Britain at the time. The 22-gun battleship had been built to prevent the Americans from gaining naval supremacy over Lake Ontario and to protect Canadian interests on the northern side of the lake.

The ship sunk on an exceptionally cold Halloween night in a sudden squall while anchored in the eastern end of the lake, near Oswego, New York. There were no survivors and no remains of the ship have ever been found, except for a barrel that washed up on shore immediately afterwards.

Reliable statistics on the number of deaths are hard to come by. Most reports say that between 172 and 350 men drowned. If the number was indeed 350, it would make the sinking of the *Ontario* the worst shipwreck ever in the Great Lakes.

A massive cargo of gold—destined to fund the ongoing British military effort—was also lost with the ship and was estimated to be worth as much as $500,000. Naval historians have blamed the *Ontario*'s design for its quick demise, suggesting that it was too flat bottomed and thus unable to properly balance itself during heavy storms on the lakes.

Today, the wreck remains the focus of a number of ghost stories. The eastern end of Lake Ontario, where it meets the St. Lawrence River, had an exceptionally bad reputation among sailors during the 18th and 19th centuries. It even became known as a sort of freshwater Bermuda Triangle, into which ships mysteriously disappeared without a trace. The area was named the "Marysburgh Vortex," after the nearby Marysburgh Township. Survivors of later shipwrecks in the area sometimes described a strange magnetic force that seemed to inexplicably pull ships off course. There were also tales of giant columns of rock that would suddenly appear, causing ships to crash—and then disappear again.

However, with the advent of metal-hulled boats, and sonar and radio communication, the eastern lake's bad reputation diminished in the 20th century. It now seems likely that the *Ontario* and other ships lost in the "Vortex" were the victims of mundane causes—ordinary storms and poor navigation and design.

Sinking of the *Speedy*

IN 1804—when Upper Canada was still a young colony—some of the most important dignitaries of that time were lost in a surprising shipwreck. The result might have changed the history of Upper Canada dramatically.

The government-owned HMS *Speedy* was a small boat, only 25 metres in length. It had been built hastily in 1798 at Kingston, to defend against an American attack.

On October 7, the boat was on a short voyage along the shore of Lake Ontario, from York to the newly formed town of Newcastle. The trip was expected to take two days.

But before the boat sailed, there were ominous signs that went unheeded.

Captain Thomas Paxton had been reluctant to set sail, given the bad weather. There had been an early cold snap, accompanied by some heavy snow. Rash decisions, unfortunately, had plagued the boat since its construction. The *Speedy* was built in such a rush, it was said, that green timber of poor quality was used. By 1804, this had already caused a number of problems, including dry rot and warping in the ship. Two men were required to constantly bail water out of the ship using bilge pumps in order to keep it afloat! Despite these problems, Governor Peter Hunter ordered Paxton and the *Speedy* to head out immediately, under penalty of court martial.

The *Speedy*'s mission was no less than the founding of Newcastle and conducting of the government's first business there, which included trials and, most likely, executions.

Until that point, Newcastle had been little more than a name on a map. Its barren cliffs and natural harbours had inspired surveyors travelling along the north shore of the lake to name a string of proposed settlements after northeastern English locations, which they thought the landscape resembled. Moving east from York (now Toronto), they named Scarborough, Pickering, Whitby and Newcastle.

Many of Upper Canada's elite preferred the location of Newcastle to that of York, and there was speculation that if the town succeeded, it might be named the new capital of Upper Canada.

On board the *Speedy* were all the men who were to oversee the founding of Newcastle, as well as a crew of surveyors and new local officials for the region. The boat also carried six handwritten copies of the Constitution of Upper Canada, which outlined the government's claims over the area.

The boat's passengers included a number of high-profile judges and other court staff from the colony's Court of Assizes, which oversaw criminal cases. They brought with them an Ojibway man, Ogetonicut, who had been accused of killing trading post operator John Sharpe, in revenge for the death of his brother. Although Ogetonicut had been arrested in York, the murder had supposedly been committed at Scugog, in the Newcastle district. Because of this, he legally had to be tried at Newcastle.

The colony's first Solicitor General, Robert Isaac Dey Gray, was on board, as was MP Angus Macdonnell, who was to act as Ogetonicut's defence attorney, and York Police Chief John Fisk. Fisk would become the first Canadian police officer killed in the line of duty.

As the *Speedy* sailed on its journey, the snow became heavier and heavier. The boat stopped at Oshawa to pick up the business partners of the murdered Sharpe, who were to stand as witnesses at the trial. The two men refused to board the ship, which they thought looked unsafe, and instead decided to follow it by canoe. However, a number of Ojibway men and women chose to join the *Speedy* in order to witness the upcoming trial of Ogetonicut.

By the time the overburdened ship approached Newcastle, on Presqu'ile Bay, a full-blown blizzard was underway. The men in the canoe managed to reach Newcastle, but the *Speedy* had disappeared. A blast from one of its cannons was heard from shore as it tried to signal its position, and a bonfire was lit to guide it safely to Newcastle. After that point, nothing more was heard from the *Speedy*. Its 40 passengers and crew members were all lost.

The next day, a chicken coop and compass box that had been on the schooner were discovered on the beach. The shallow, sandy bottom of the lake near Presqu'ile revealed no secrets. No other sign of the wreck was seen until 1836, when part of the ship and some human remains were found at Presqu'ile Bay.

Although there are plenty of explanations for the *Speedy*'s demise—including the weather, overcrowding and poor construction—people still talk about other causes. Some blame the mysterious Marysburgh Vortex area, which was said to cause pillars of rock to appear from nowhere and destroy ships. Others speculate that a fight took place between Ojibway and European passengers. Still others say that a scheme was concocted by powerful York-based business interests to sink the boat in order to prevent the successful development of Newcastle.

Indeed, the immediate blame for the sinking of the *Speedy* fell on the harbour of Newcastle itself. It was declared to be too dangerous to pilot ships through, and the town was quickly abandoned. The few buildings that had already been constructed decayed into the ground, and the site is now part of Presqu'ile Provincial Park, near Brighton. The capital of the Newcastle district was moved to Amherst (now Cobourg), and the district was later broken up into the counties of Quinte, Northumberland and Peterborough. The modern-day port of Newcastle, located close to Oshawa, is unrelated to its original and was founded in 1856.

We can continue to wonder what might have been if the *Speedy* had made its way safely to its destination. Might Newcastle, not Toronto, be the capital of Ontario and the biggest city in Canada today?

Sinking of the *General Hamilton* and *Scourge*

ANIMOSITY WAS HIGH DURING THE YEARS between the American Revolution and the War of 1812. Ontario—or Upper Canada as it was known then—had been created as a homeland for Loyalists, pro-British Americans who had opposed the Revolution. Although Britain and the United States officially made peace in 1783, peace did not immediately happen in practice. In the remote backwoods of the Great Lakes, British and American soldiers and sailors continued to fight small battles, and the lakes remained in a state of unofficial war. The Americans were particularly upset by rumours that Britain was secretly supplying weapons to hostile Aboriginal nations on land claimed by the U.S.

The *Scourge,* which was built in Niagara-on-the-Lake for a local Loyalist merchant, was originally known as the *Lord Nelson*. It had been captured by the Americans before the outbreak of the War of 1812, allegedly for engaging in arms smuggling in American waters. The *General Hamilton* had been the American merchant ship *Diana,* but the U.S. Navy had purchased it and changed its name. When the war began, both boats were converted into warships and put into service by the Americans under the command of Commodore Isaac Chauncey.

On August 8, 1813, in the second year of the War of 1812 (which actually lasted three years, despite its name), the two schooners were preparing for an attack on the British fleet at Kingston harbour. They were anchored in

Canadian waters at the mouth of Ten Mile Creek, not far from St. Catharines.

At approximately 2 AM, a sudden, isolated squall struck the two boats and sunk them almost instantly. Commodore Chauncey reported that a dozen or so sailors escaped on lifeboats and were saved. The remaining men, approximately 100 in total, drowned.

Ned Myers, a sailor on the *Scourge* who survived the sinking, later reported that it had happened so fast that most of the men could not get on deck in time to jump off. No order to abandon ship was given. Converting the ship for naval use had necessitated a much bigger crew than what it had been designed for as a trading vessel. The single hatch leading up to the deck meant that only one man could climb out at a time.

It's not clear exactly how the ships sunk. Myers reported that the *Scourge* had tilted far to one side and began taking on water. As he prepared to jump into the lake, he heard the voice of another sailor shouting "Don't jump overboard! Don't jump overboard! The schooner is righting!" But Myers went ahead and jumped anyway. He believed that the ship sunk the moment that he jumped, taking with it the sailor who had shouted the warning. Myers was able to find a lifeboat and rescued a number of other men who were drowning in the water.

The storm disappeared without a trace almost as soon as it came. British ships in Lake Ontario did not learn about the disaster until three days later when they captured an American ship that had picked up some of the survivors.

The sinking of the two ships proved to be the worst military shipwreck of the War of 1812.

The *General Hamilton* and *Scourge* remained at the bottom of the lake undiscovered until the late 20th century.

In 1972, Dr. Daniel Nelson, a dentist and amateur historian from St. Catharines, became interested in locating the wrecks of the ships. He used the logs from other War of 1812 ships to pinpoint the possible location of the sinking. In 1975, with the help of the Royal Ontario Museum, he was able to use sonar to identify the ships. The ships remained the property of the U.S. Navy until 1979, at which time the Canadian government negotiated for their ownership to be transferred. Famous French underwater explorer Jacques Cousteau visited the wrecks in 1980 and helped photograph them, and *National Geographic* magazine featured them in 1982.

Both ships turned out to be remarkably intact and well preserved. They were identified by their figureheads, which still recall the ships' original names: the Greek goddess Diana, and the famous admiral, Lord Nelson. Divers have photographed the decks, masts, guns and unused lifeboats. The skeletal remains of at least six sailors on the decks of the doomed vessels were also identified.

It is perhaps appropriate then that a legend in the St. Catharines area holds that on stormy summer nights, the ghostly images of the two sinking ships can still be seen and the screams of their crews heard.

Cholera Outbreaks

═══════════ ❧◆❧ ═══════════

1832 and 1834
York (Toronto)

CHOLERA WAS A DEADLY DISEASE that gained wide attention in the 19th century. It originated in India, around the Ganges River, and spread outwards, carried by travelling merchants and soldiers.

At a time when cities in Europe and North America were notorious for poor sanitation, cholera was especially devastating. The disease was rarely passed from one person to another; instead, it was usually contracted through drinking polluted water. Unfortunately, this important fact was not yet known. Few urban people—even the wealthy—had access to clean water in those days, and many wells were contaminated by sewage, including waste from cholera patients. The bacteria could also be transmitted by consuming poorly cooked fish or shellfish.

Virtually all water, even today, contains small amounts of the *Vibrio cholerae* bacteria that causes cholera, usually contained within plankton. However, it takes a significant amount of the bacteria to do damage to an otherwise healthy person. In the 19th century, not only was sanitation and water treatment poor, but many people were already suffering from other health problems and malnutrition. This compounded the effect of the bacteria.

A healthy person would need to swallow approximately one million bacteria in order to catch cholera. Although that may seem a large amount, a single cup of polluted water could contain that much bacteria. (The Russian composer Pyotr Tchaikovsky is said to have died one day after drinking a glass of contaminated water from a well in St. Petersburg—it was thought to be a deliberate suicide.) After being swallowed, the bacteria would have to survive the acidity of the stomach before moving on to the lower intestine, where it would spread to the rest of the body.

Interestingly, susceptibility to cholera was also determined by blood type. People with the blood type AB were the least susceptible, whereas those with O—the most common type—were the most susceptible.

Cholera reached Canada in 1832, brought by immigrants from Europe. The government had set up Grosse Île, near Québec City, as a massive quarantine station for new immigrants, but the system was chaotic and badly enforced. Many healthy immigrants were left on Grosse Île, where they became sick and died, but other sick newcomers were allowed in, where they infected the population.

Serious outbreaks of cholera occurred across Ontario in 1832, most devastatingly in York (which was renamed Toronto in 1834). York had a mere 15 doctors for a population of over 6000. In surrounding areas, medical help was even harder to come by.

In that same year, 40,000 new immigrants arrived in York within a single summer. Blame for the spread of cholera in York was quickly put on the newcomers, most of whom came from England. But it was the cesspools of York itself that caused the disease to spread.

The city was a notoriously unsanitary place, as was noted by one visitor who said, "Stagnant pools of water, green as a leek and emitting deadly exhalations are to be met with in every corner of the town—yards and cellars send forth a stench already from rotten vegetables sufficient almost of itself to produce a plague—and the state of the bay, from which a large proportion of the inhabitants are supplied with water, is horrible."

In early 1832, there was no public health legislation in Upper Canada. Unfortunately, attempts to block the spread of cholera fell prey to political tension between the colony's government and opposition groups. Rather than recognizing the crisis and working together to stop it, politicians treated cholera as just another topic to do battle on. This continued the tradition of hostility between the British-appointed governor and the elite of Upper Canada on one hand, and William Lyon Mackenzie's radicals on the other.

The authorities attempted to stop immigrants from entering the colony by setting up roadblocks between towns. Mackenzie was highly skeptical of these efforts, which he saw as just another attempt by the government to restrict the freedom of Upper Canadians. He also believed that the development of a public health bureaucracy would do little more than provide jobs for friends of the government. In his newspaper, the *Colonial Advocate,* Mackenzie often made fun of the fears expressed by doctors regarding the threat of cholera. It's likely that he borrowed most of his views on cholera from the Radical movement in England, which believed the government had created a panic to keep ordinary citizens in their place.

Limited public health legislation was passed on June 28, 1832, by Mackenzie's Tory opponents—the same day as the colony's first cholera case was reported in York. The legislation allowed public money to be spent on supplying the poor with lime dust, which they could use to kill bacteria in their houses. Money was also made available to pay for horses and carts to take the sick to the hospital.

Those poor citizens who died in York's public hospital were buried in unmarked graves on unconsecrated ground, which caused a controversy. Potter's Field, at the corner of Bloor and Yonge streets, was purchased by the government during the epidemic and became York's first secular graveyard. A plaque marks its spot today.

(It is interesting to note that "potter's fields" appeared in cities across Europe and North America as places to bury the poor. The name is a biblical reference to Judas, who, after receiving a reward for betraying Christ, was consumed by guilt and hanged himself. But before doing this, he donated the reward money to a temple, which used it to buy a field as a burying site for unknown travellers. The place was called "potter's field" because the land was considered only good for harvesting clay for pottery.)

In the end, however, little was done to improve the sanitation of the city, and severely polluted wells and water systems went unfixed. Many residents simply locked themselves in their houses and refused to go outside during the worst days of the cholera outbreak.

Cholera raged in York and other cities in the colony from June to September of 1832, leading to 273 officially reported deaths (historians estimate that the real number was probably closer to 500). An average of 10 citizens of York died every day at the height of the outbreak, a low figure when compared with the much greater number of deaths in Montréal, which were estimated to be as high as 3000.

Outside of York, individual towns were often forced to go it alone against the disease. Most ports refused to allow ships to dock unless a doctor had inspected them. This measure reassured locals but often infuriated ship captains and owners.

One particularly regretful incident involving a ship took place in July 1832. The steamship *Canada* managed to run a municipal inspection blockade on July 3. By July 5, however, its captain reluctantly allowed the local medical officer, Dr. Porter, to begin inspecting the ship. But after Porter left, the ship continued to steam towards Niagara (now Niagara-on-the-Lake). Porter was irritated by the captain's unwillingness to cooperate and ordered him to stop the ship before it reached Niagara so that the inspection could be finished. On July 7, the inspection still wasn't complete, and the captain decided to push on for Niagara despite the doctor's order.

Dr. Porter hailed the *Canada* as it arrived, but the ship refused to stop. As its crew attempted to tie it up at the wharf, an angry mob from Niagara attacked them, shouting "We are not going to be infected!" The crowd tried to bludgeon the sailors, and a huge running fight broke out when the crew of the nearby *Great Britain* came ashore to help the *Canada*'s crew. The captain of the *Canada* claimed that Dr. Porter had climbed on top of the *Great Britain*, where he cheered on "the lowest orders of Niagara." The riot—which was almost certainly related to the hostile political factions in the colony—could not be stopped until the army put it down.

The fear caused by the cholera outbreak prompted many Upper Canada residents to take solace in religion. The Methodist church reported 3652 conversions in 1832, three times the number of the previous year.

Although the cholera outbreak declined by the end of 1832, it made a resurgence in the summer of 1834. This time, little public information about the disease was made available. The government of Lower Canada (modern-day Québec) had decided that all the news of the 1832 epidemic had made for negative press in the region. They feared businesses would suffer if cholera's return was publicized and wanted to avoid the controversy that would follow the publication of an official death count. Many in Upper Canada were surprised to find the deadly disease on them again, not having heard about the outbreak in Lower Canada.

In 1834, the former city of York—newly incorporated as Toronto—had 500 cholera deaths on its hands.

The disease disappeared for good later that year. Although some new hospital facilities were built and improvements to public health regulations were made, Toronto's water and sewage systems remained incomplete and dangerously flawed. And it was not until 1849 that the work of Dr. John Snow in England showed a definite link between polluted water and cholera.

Typhus Epidemic

IN 1847, TORONTO WAS OVERWHELMED by a wave of Irish immigration. The city's population was only 20,000, but in that year alone, 38,000 Irish refugees arrived, mostly by boat. They were fleeing the disastrous Irish famine, in which as many as a million people starved to death between 1846 and 1849.

An outbreak of typhus spread among the starving, impoverished refugees. Thousands died aboard ships crossing the Atlantic, and 3000 died while in quarantine on Québec's infamous Grosse Île. So many people caught the disease on route to North America that it was nick-named "ship fever." One-fifth of all those fleeing the famine are estimated to have died of typhus. Those who got past Grosse Île headed inland, to Montréal, or Toronto.

Whereas many of the earlier Irish immigrants to Toronto had been Protestant, these immigrants were mostly Catholic. This only increased the poor reception they received in a city that was so Protestant-dominated that it had become known as "Methodist Rome."

"Irish beggars are to be met everywhere, and they are as ignorant and vicious as they are poor," wrote Liberal politician George Brown in *The Globe* newspaper, which he founded. "They are lazy, improvident, and unthankful; they fill our poorhouses and our prisons, and are as brutish in their superstition as Hindoos [sic]."

Although the majority of the Irish immigrants who arrived in Toronto that year headed outward to smaller towns, many were so crippled with illness that they were unable to leave the city. Toronto's health care system was simply unable to handle so many sick people.

The old Toronto General Hospital, built in 1820—the only hospital in the city at the time—was quickly over-whelmed. Indeed, the hospital was forced to shut its doors and relocate to a larger building, but even this was insuf-ficient. Crude wooden barracks—known as "fever sheds"—were built on the site of the old hospital to house the patients in the worst condition or those unable to afford proper care. The grouping of fever sheds was called, sarcastically, "The Emigrant Hospital." Most of its "patients" died. Another health care centre, the Conva-lescent Hospital, was built at the foot of Bathurst Street to allow healthier recovery from the disease. It dealt with 300 patients daily.

One of the most shocking recorded stories of typhus deaths concerned the Willis family from County Limerick, Ireland. The whole family, which included two parents and five children, had been preparing to leave for Canada to escape the famine. One of the children became sick as the family waited to board the ship and had to be left behind to die in Ireland. Two of the children died while the ship was crossing the Atlantic. A fourth child died in quarantine on Grosse Île, leaving only the parents and one child. The family landed in Québec City and headed for Toronto, from where they went on to Brantford and eventually London. In London, the father and the one remaining child also died.

Torontonians had never seen this sort of outbreak before, and panic soon took hold. All immigrant ships were forced to dock at Rees' Pier so that a doctor could examine each immigrant. Those found to be sick were quarantined in the fever sheds. Even the fever sheds themselves caused fear. When some construction workers became sick after adding extensions to the sheds, other construction workers went on strike.

Ultimately, 1100 people died of typhus in Toronto in 1847, nearly all of them Irish immigrants. Hundreds more died in the small fever shed compounds in Kingston and London.

Of the few Torontonians who made courageous efforts to help the sick, some ended up with the disease themselves. The city's chief medical officer, George Grasset, died on July 18. Michael Power, the city's first Catholic archbishop, died on October 1.

Many of the immigrants who died had arrived alone and therefore had no one to identify them or pay for their funerals. These people were buried in unmarked mass graves in front of St. Paul's Basilica, St. James Cathedral and St. Michael's Cathedral.

As occurs in many disasters, unscrupulous people took advantage wherever they could. Locals were shocked when they saw a hearse, on route to St. Paul's, overturn on King Street. A coffin fell out of it and broke open, revealing not one, but two bodies. Placing two bodies in one coffin was specifically against city bylaws, suggesting that someone was cutting corners. It was thought that Thomas Ryan, the undertaker commissioned by the Emigrant Hospital's managers, was trying to save money. St. Paul's Basilica charged him 10 shillings for each coffin he deposited into the mass grave. The hospital also could have been trying to save money by ordering fewer coffins. Since the government offered the hospital money to cover the burial of each typhus victim, corrupt hospital managers may have pocketed the difference.

The local Irish newspaper, the *Mirror,* blamed relief workers for the corruption and accused them of pilfering government funds through a number of schemes.

One of the most shocking details of the whole typhus outbreak is how easily it could have been prevented. The disease, caused by the *Rickettsia prowazekii* bacteria, was traditionally associated with poverty ("typhus" comes from *typhos,* the Greek word for "lazy"). Once infected, a patient would not start to see symptoms for a week. After that, they would begin to experience fever, headaches, chills, exhaustion, and break out in a rash. These would be followed by enlargement of the liver and spleen, and then death.

Typhus was typically hosted by rats or mice and transmitted to humans by lice—specifically through louse feces. The lice connection was not discovered until 1909, by French bacteriologist Charles Nicolle. He discovered that patients in the early stages of typhus could be cured with a simple hot bath and change of clothes. It was the dense living quarters and unsanitary conditions of the ships, Grosse Île and the fever sheds that had massively exacerbated typhus.

A vaccine for the disease was completed in 1938 and released in 1943.

A memorial to the victims of typhus still stands today in front of St. Paul's Basilica, above the mass grave. Another memorial was unveiled in 2007 at the south end of Bathurst Street.

Shannonville Train Wreck

───── ❖ ─────

June 22, 1872
Shannonville (Quinte County)

TRAIN CONDUCTOR HENRY NEILSON was in the first-class car answering a passenger's question. Luckily enough, because he had moved from his usual post, Neilson survived what was to be a bloody and devastating crash. He went on to lead the rescue efforts that followed the Shannonville wreck.

At 1 AM, on June 22, 1873, an overnight Grand Trunk Railway passenger train derailed. It had been on its way to Toronto from Montréal and was passing Shannonville, just east of Belleville. The train was running 20 minutes behind schedule but picked up speed while passing by the Salmon River embankment. Passengers reported a violent swaying motion, just before the train heaved over the edge of the embankment.

The engine rolled off the track, dragging the baggage car past it. The second-class car telescoped, then fell immediately on top of the engine. It damaged the engine's steam tank, breaking it open and scalding the passengers with boiling steam. Within half a minute, many had been boiled alive by the steam, in some cases actually breathing it in. Indeed, the steam caused more deaths than the actual derailment.

The first-class coaches derailed but were not seriously damaged, while the sleeper car survived without any damage.

A telegram was immediately sent to Belleville, calling for every available doctor. Meanwhile, Neilson led the rescue, along with businessman Robert Roddy, a passenger on the train. The two men used crowbars to free the injured from the wreckage, and the sleeping car was made into a first aid station.

In all, 34 passengers and crew died.

Dr. Burdett, one of the medical professionals to arrive on the scene, later organized a coroner's inquest. The disaster was chalked up to bad luck, blaming a "flange breaking on a right-hand wheel on the locomotive's front truck."

Besides causing the tragic loss of the lives, the crash had serious political ramifications. The Grand Trunk Railway was closely associated with Conservative Prime Minister Sir John A. Macdonald, and its safety record had a major effect on his career. On the one hand, Liberal-affiliated newspapers, like the *Daily Globe*, lined up to condemn the railway. They labelled the inquest a farce and alleged that most of the witnesses were being paid by the railway company. On the other hand, Conservative papers, like the *Toronto Mail*, joined the debate in favour of the Grand Trunk Railway.

A second inquiry was held, which placed most of the blame on the engineer, along with the broken wheel mentioned in the first inquiry. The exact cause of the broken wheel was never determined. Expert witnesses disagreed as to how much of a role the track's condition had played in the crash. Engineer John Henry Dumble testified that the rail spikes were loose, which may have caused the track to shake and thus derail the train. However, it was noted that a rescue train had passed over the area only an hour after the accident and had encountered no problems.

Komoka Train Wreck

SIX KILOMETRES FROM KOMOKA—a town that has since become a suburb of London—fire broke out in a washroom of a Great Western Railway car on February 28, 1874. The coal-oil lamp in the washroom had either exploded or dropped, quickly catching fire to the wooden frame of the car.

The train's conductor, John Mitchell, noticed a commotion coming from the car. He assumed that some of the passengers were having a fight. In fact, they were struggling to put out the fire, using the cushions and blankets from their sleeping births. Mitchell attempted to calm down the passengers, but panic broke out as they desperately tried to extinguish the fire on the speeding train.

Instead of closing the door of the washroom and evacuating to other cars—which might have saved them—frenzied passengers began rushing at the washroom, trying unsuccessfully to put out the flames. The fire soon spread out across the car, trapping passengers at the back of the train.

Attempts were made to uncouple the burning car, to save the rest of the train and to allow passengers to jump off more easily, but the coupler refused to give.

Mitchell soon realized that he had to act quickly in order to stop the train. His efforts to do this, however, were made more difficult because he was unable to communicate with the engineer. A number of freight cars were in between the engine and the passenger cars, and the noise of the cars was too much to shout over.

Laws had earlier been passed to force all trains to have a "bell rope," which a conductor could pull to warn the engineer of danger. However, these laws were generally ignored when trains mixed freight and passengers cars together. The dangerous implications of this policy had apparently not been realized previously.

Mitchell was forced to climb along the side of the freight cars until he got close enough to the engine so that he could shout to the engineer to stop the train. The train finally came to a stop 4 kilometres from Komoka.

Many passengers were injured after desperately jumping from the moving train to avoid the fire. Still others were injured from the fire itself or from smoke inhalation. In total, seven people died in the fire, including a mother and her three-year-old child. Another three people later died in hospital.

An inquest into the disaster began on March 2. Of particular concern were the lamp and the problems with uncoupling the car, as well as the lack of a bell rope. The inquest recommended that oil lamps be banned from train cars and that laws around bell ropes be strictly adhered to. It further recommended that all the train's staff—including Mitchell—be charged with manslaughter.

A grand jury under Justice Joseph C. Morrison—a former Great Western Railway lawyer—dropped the charges against the men. The decision outraged the families of many of the victims, who believed Morrison was secretly still in the pay of the railway.

A number of civil suits followed the decision. Passenger Ebenezer Hooper was awarded $250 for minor injuries. Hugh Munro, who suffered debilitating injuries, sued for $10,000. The Great Western Railway was willing to offer $450 to Munro, but a jury awarded him $1450— about two years' salary. Another man, who had lost his 17-year-old daughter in the crash, attempted to sue for $1000 but lost.

Sinking of the *Waubuno*

SAILORS ARE FAMOUSLY SUPERSTITIOUS—not surprising for a vocation whose practitioners' lives often depend on luck alone. Hundreds of nautical superstitions exist, regarding weather, birds and fish, and ships' names.

That considered, the *Waubuno* was an odd name indeed. "Waubuno" is said to be an Ojibway word meaning "black magic."

A lumber company owned the *Waubuno* during the heyday of the logging on Georgian Bay. As well as lumber and supplies, the wooden propeller boat often carried passengers around the bay. However, the *Waubuno* was 14 years old. She was beginning to show her age and could not sail as quickly as the newer ships. *Magnettawan*, a ship owned by a rival lumber company that travelled the same route, frequently beat *Waubuno* to their destination. Captain Burkett's employers often complained that he was not moving *Waubuno* fast enough.

The pressure to outrun *Magnettawan* might explain why Burkett decided to leave dock at Owen Sound at 4 AM on November 22. The ship was not scheduled to leave for several hours, so not all of the passengers were even on board yet. *Waubuno*'s destination was Parry Sound, towards the northeast end of Georgian Bay. On that fateful day, *Waubuno* did indeed get ahead of her younger rival *Magnettawan*. Unfortunately, the ship never made it to Parry Sound.

One of the ship's passengers who did make it aboard was Mrs. Douse, a young woman recently married to a doctor in Parry Sound. She was set to join him and begin a new life in the port town. The night before the voyage, she told her friends that she had had a vivid nightmare of the *Waubuno* sinking in a storm—but nobody took heed.

The morning of November 22 was characterized by an intense snowstorm that swept over Georgian Bay. Both *Waubuno* and *Magnettawan* diverted their course to the area of Christian Island, near the bay's southeastern end. However, while *Magnettawan* decided to dock there and wait some 40 hours for the weather to improve, *Waubuno* pushed on. The ship was last sighted by the lighthouse keeper on Christian Island, sailing north into the storm.

That afternoon, lumberjacks who were north of Christian Island at Moose Point heard the sounds of a distress call—presumably from the *Waubuno*—but did not recognize it as such. What happened next is not known. Historians surmised that Captain Burkett had taken the ship north of Moose Point but was forced to turn back because of the heavy snow. Although an excellent navigator, Burkett apparently didn't know about the shoal—known today as the Haystacks—off Moose Point. The *Waubuno* probably hit the shoal and was forced to drop its anchors in an attempt to stop the storm from sweeping it away. However, the anchors did not hold, and the ship likely was swept away and dashed to pieces.

All 24 people on board were lost: 10 passengers and 14 crew.

Two days later, on November 24, the tugboat *Mittie Grew* discovered parts of *Waubuno* and overturned lifeboats floating off Moose Point. All the ship's lifejackets were found—a sign that the tragedy happened very quickly, not giving the crew and passengers time to prepare.

It is likely that a heavy wave struck the ship and filled it with water, pulling it down into the lake. Passersby reported seeing barrels of flour and other supplies floating in the water, as well as portions of the cabin and top deck.

Most of the ship's hull washed up, upside down, on an island near Parry Sound the following spring. It was not until 1959 that divers discovered the rest of the wreck. In 1962, they hauled up its anchor and placed it in the town square of Parry Sound, where it still sits today.

The sinking of the *Waubuno* left a mark on the names of locations in Georgian Bay. The rocky entrance to Parry Sound where Captain Burkett probably turned back is now known as the Waubuno Channel. The place where the hull washed up is known as Wreck Island, and the specific part of the Haystacks that the ship probably came aground on is called Burkett's Rock.

Sinking of the *Jane Miller*

November 26, 1881
Georgian Bay (Lake Huron)

ONE OF THE MANY SHIPS TO DISAPPEAR into a November snow-storm in Ontario was the *Jane Miller*. In its two years of existence, the ship had serviced many ports of Georgian Bay, transporting both supplies and passengers. The wooden propeller boat was on route from Meaford to Wiarton, both located at the southern end of the bay.

The short journey was probably what convinced Captain Port and his crew to push ahead, despite the inclement weather. The *Jane Miller* had picked up extra cargo at Meaford, and this plus a lack of ballast had made the ship dangerously top-heavy.

Almost nothing is known of the last journey of the *Jane Miller*. The ship was spotted from shore but appeared to be stationary at the time. The witness who reported seeing it stated that a huge gust of snow obscured his vision of the ship after that. He did not see it again.

A rescue ship was sent out after the *Jane Miller*, but it found only bubbles and discoloured water rising up from the place where the ship was last seen. Its 28 passengers and crew were presumed dead.

No bodies were ever discovered, though a few items from the *Jane Miller* were later found washed up on White Cloud Island in Colpoy's Bay. These included some kegs of butter with the captain's name printed on them, a broken flagstaff, cradles for the lifeboats, oars with the ship's name, and uniform caps that had belonged to the crew.

The lack of remains could be explained by the ship's top-heaviness. It is possible that the *Jane Miller* simply flipped over in the storm, filled with water and sunk, pulling all those aboard down with it.

An editorial in the *Wiarton Echo* concluded, "That not one of the victims of the disaster has been found need not be wondered at, when it is considered that the strong gale and snow storm which was raging at the time, no doubt compelled every gangway and other avenue of escape to be closed against the elements without. Thus, completely penned in, and before the slightest effort could be made to save themselves, twenty-eight souls were hurled into eternity without time to utter a prayer."

The tragedy was further recorded by the *Cleveland Herald*, which wrote, "Captain Port was recognized as a most skillful officer, and a man of superior judgment in handling his craft. He leaves a wife and family of grown up children. The engineer, Christison, also leaves a family."

Some attempts have been made to locate the wreck of the *Jane Miller*, but at some 60 metres below the surface, at the rocky bottom of Colpoy's Bay, it remains outside the range of most divers. As a result, its exact location is still a mystery. In 1968, the Ontario government dedicated a plaque to the ship in Wiarton.

Sinking of the *Asia*

ONE THE WORST SHIPWRECKS IN THE GREAT LAKES occurred in a typical lake squall in 1882. It brought down the sizable all-purpose ship, *Asia*, which was only nine years old and had been built at the tremendous cost of $25,000.

The wreck left all but two of its 97 passengers and 28 crew members dead. It is from one of those survivors, a teenager named Dunkan Tinkiss who later told his story to the *Meaford Monitor*, that we have an account of the events of the disaster. Seventeen-year-old Christy Anne Morrison also survived.

The *Asia* was on a voyage from Presqu'ile to French River. It had docked in Owen Sound and was on the final leg of its journey across Georgian Bay. The ship carried a mixed cargo of logging equipment and provisions as well as horses. The *Asia* suffered a night of heavy rain and high winds. The passengers' area filled with broken china and debris, knocked around by the turbulent waves. Tinkiss' uncle, also on board the ship, predicted that it would go down.

The captain found matters even worse in the morning. He tried to steer the ship towards the safety of Lonely Island, but it foundered off Byng Inlet instead. Stranded in the midst of the storm with its engines still working, the ship was hit by two huge waves that tipped it starboard and broke it into pieces.

Tinkiss was able to get on deck before the ship went down, and he swam for one of the lifeboats, where the ship's purser pulled him in. Eighteen people were crammed into the lifeboat. Tinkiss had the awful experience of watching one crew member after another die as they were washed overboard by waves or died from exposure.

The lifeboat overturned several times during the storm. In the first such incident, the purser who had helped Tinkiss was swept into the lake. The cabin boy was also washed overboard, and the boat-hand, who had jumped into the water, was not seen again. Another four men died in the boat that night. The captain died in Tinkiss' arms the morning after the wreck. Only Tinkiss and Morrison remained alive.

The two teenagers were not able to navigate the boat, which was badly damaged and missing its oars, but they floated towards land. They approached Pointe au Baril in the Thirty Thousand Islands, but they had no idea where they were. The pair landed the boat on the beach and laid out the bodies of the others who had died during the journey.

Their night on the beach was spent in feverish dreams; Tinkiss kept reliving the horror of the wreck in his mind. He and Morrison were almost too weak to move, soaked in water, starving and cold.

The next day, they finally saw the shape of a sail approaching them. At first, Tinkiss was so delirious that he believed it was a large schooner. In fact, it was only a little mackinaw (a broad canoe with a sail, popular in the Great Lakes). The single occupant of the mackinaw, an Ojibway fisherman, offered them some pork and hard "chock dog" cheese, which Tinkiss said was "the best meal I ever had in my life."

Believing that they were on the opposite side of Georgian Bay, Tinkiss asked the fisherman to take them to Manitoulin Island. However, the island was much too far for the fisherman to go. Tinkiss and Morrison were

Christy Ann Morrison, one of the two survivors of the sinking of the *Asia* in Georgian Bay in 1882.

actually closer to the *Asia*'s intended destination on the eastern shore of Georgian Bay. The fisherman dropped them off in Parry Sound, from where the two were able to make their way home.

An inquiry into the sinking of the *Asia* concluded that it was not heavily weighted enough with cargo and, in particular, was too light forwards. As a result, the ship wasn't properly balanced and could be toppled over too easily.

Despite thorough searches, both at the time and recently, the wreck of the *Asia* has never been found.

Sinking of the *Mary Ann Hulbert*

THE SINKING OF THE *MARY ANN HULBERT* is the story of an awful sacrifice. The barge was being towed across Lake Superior by the steamer *Kincardine*, transporting 15 railway workers and 5 crew members. The two ships were travelling from Michipicoten Island to Port Arthur (now part of Thunder Bay). Although it was late in the year for any sort of heavy shipping to take place, the railway company that owned the ships was keen to get the team of workers to the western end of the lake as soon as possible.

As often occurs with Great Lakes disasters, the *Kincardine* and *Hulbert* were hit by a heavy snowstorm that came without warning. Sometime around midnight, between November 14 and 15, things came to a dangerous climax. The *Hulbert*'s crew were young and inexperienced when it came to dealing with snow squalls. As a result, they had difficulty handling the barge, and it began to whip back and forth, threatening the stability of both ships.

The crew of the *Kincardine* decided that they had only one option: to cut the cables that connected it to the *Hulbert* so that the ship could manoeuvre itself properly. They could only hope that the barge would safely drift to shore.

Unsurprisingly, this decision boded badly for the *Hulbert*. After being severed from the steamer, it quickly sprung a leak and was sucked under the waves. The *Kincardine* attempted to search for survivors, but the continuing storm forced it to head for port.

No survivors or remains of the *Mary Ann Hulbert* have ever been found.

Sinking of the *Algoma*

November 7, 1885
Lake Superior

THE GREAT LAKES MUST HAVE SEEMED little more than a large bathtub to the crew of the *Algoma*. After all, they had already sailed the ship across the Atlantic Ocean!

The *Algoma* was built in 1883 in Glasgow, Scotland, along with her sister ships *Athabasca* and *Alberta*. Apparently the three vessels were extremely well constructed and more advanced in design than the ships being built in North America at the time. They were also the first ships on the Great Lakes that had electrical lighting—a huge advantage when it came to sailing through storms and foggy conditions.

The Canadian Pacific Railway (CPR), in this era of massive rail expansion, had commissioned all three ships. The Atlantic and Pacific coasts of Canada were being connected by railways, and new branches were being built to service mining and logging towns in northern Ontario. Together, the ships would bring tonnes of railway equipment, machinery, cars and steam engines, as well as hundreds of workers, to remote depots across the Great Lakes.

The CPR avoided no expense in building the ships and bringing them to Canada. At the time, the Lachine Rapids and the narrowness of the St. Lawrence River and Welland Canal meant that large ships could not sail directly through to Lake Erie. After being sailed to Montréal, the ships were disassembled and brought by train to Port Colbourne on Lake Erie, where they were put back together again.

While doing this, it soon became obvious to the CPR that there was an untapped market for transporting passengers in the upper Great Lakes. Soon, *Algoma* and other ships similar to her began to carry large numbers of passengers.

The ship was 80-metres long and could carry up to 1500 passengers and 65,000 bushels of grain. Luckily, on her fateful final voyage, there were only a few passengers on board. Most of the ship's capacity had been filled with the 134 tonnes of railway supplies it was hauling.

The *Algoma* became caught in a heavy storm while it was journeying between Owen Sound and Port Arthur (now part of Thunder Bay). By November 7, it was most of the way across Lake Superior, nearing its destination.

The waves and blinding snow became so heavy that it was impossible to see from one end of the steamer to the other. The passengers on board were deeply alarmed. Despite the efforts of Captain Moore and his crew to calm them down, they began to scream and pray loudly.

Moore decided to steer the boat towards Rock Harbor on Isle Royale, a large island on the American side of the lake, just south of Port Arthur. However, the dangers posed by rocky shoals around the harbour soon became clear. Moore eventually decided to pull back out into the open lake, but his decision came too late. Just as the *Algoma* turned around and headed outwards, it was hit by a huge wave that smashed it into the rocks.

After hours of tossing and turning, the ship became eerily still. Passengers rushed the cabin, demanding that Moore tell them what had just happened. "We are on a reef," he replied, "but if you will only keep as calm as possible I trust all will be safely landed." Indeed, Moore had reason to be hopeful; they were stuck, but the shore was less than 20 metres away.

Just as he had spoken these words, a crew member came up from below to report that the steel bottom of the boat had been punctured and water was coming in.

Moore quickly rushed to ready the lifeboats and was about to lower them into the water when another wave hit the *Algoma*. The first mate was holding on to one female passenger and her daughter, but the force of the wave swept all three of them overboard. A number of male passengers disobeyed the captain's orders and jumped overboard after them—never to be seen again. The crew headed up the riggings. The wave had pushed the *Algoma* off the rocks again. It swept the ship outwards and flipped it over. The passengers and crew were thrown into the frothy, icy water as the blizzard and high winds continued.

A few people—including Captain Moore—managed to climb into one of the lifeboats. Using a plank of wood— since the oars had been washed away—Moore was able to row them towards Isle Royale. The winds and waves were so strong that they were forced to strap themselves to the lifeboat. Just as the lifeboat approached the island, it flipped over, and its passengers believed that they were done for.

However, by that point, the water was shallow enough that they could touch the bottom, and they were able to walk ashore. There they waited, from 10 AM until the late afternoon, soaking wet in the heavy snow. None of them spoke very much during those hours. Mostly they just huddled together and stared silently and anxiously at one another. Moore led them in prayer. Eventually, they were picked up by the *Athabaska*, with the help of fishermen from Isle Royale. The fishermen called the storm the worst they had ever seen. They reported that the waves had been so strong that their deep water nets had been shredded and thrown back on to shore.

The wrecked hulk of the massive Canadian Pacific Railway ship, *Algoma*. It was lost after striking a reef in Lake Superior in 1885.

CPR sent tugboats out to search the water and the shores of Isle Royale for any remaining survivors. None were found. In all, between 37 and 48 passengers were lost (the passenger list was lost with the ship, so no exact number of the dead is known). Among the sailors who drowned was the nephew of Prime Minister Alexander Mackenzie.

A crowd waited at the docks of Port Arthur to see the survivors, a majority of whom had to be carried to the hospital. Fourteen people survived, most of them severely injured. Captain Moore had been nearly crushed by the roof of the cabin as it collapsed onto him. The first and second mates had their feet badly cut by broken glass when the ship's windows shattered, and all had frostbite over their bodies.

William R. McCarter, a passenger, was another of the survivors. He and his neighbour William Mulligan had left their homes in Meaford and were going to British Columbia with the idea of settling there. Mulligan was among the dead.

McCarter told his story to the *Meaford Monitor:*

> *A stranger stopped me and said: "This is a terrible occurrence. It is sad to think we must all die here. Let us hope it will turn out all right." This poor man was drowned in less than a quarter of an hour after. The men from down below all crowded upon the higher deck and along the port side. The storm was terrible. The waves rushing in great mountains over the decks, and every few minutes the despairing shriek of some unfortunate persons was heard as they were carried out to sea and lost… The man on the other side received a severe blow on his head and cried out: "I'm crushed, I'm gone!" The next great wave carried him off without the slightest struggle, and he went to death without a groan. The night was terrible. No on can ever imagine what the people must have endured.*

The wreck of the *Algoma* represented the biggest disaster in the history of the CPR. However, it was overshadowed by another event. On the same day the ship went down, the "golden spike" was hammered in. The railway had finally connected the Atlantic and Pacific oceans.

Great Lakes Storm of 1905

ONE OF THE WORST SERIES OF SQUALLS on the Great Lakes wrecked 111 ships on both sides of the U.S./Canada border in 1905. A total of 14 steel carriers—thought capable of surviving the worst weather at the time—were beached on the shores of Lake Superior and Lake Huron.

The Canadian vessel *Minnedosa* was the largest sail ship ever to sail the Great Lakes. It had been built in Kingston in 1890 and was on its way from Fort William (now Thunder Bay) to Kingston. For six years, the ship had been taking the same route from Lake Superior to Lake Ontario—at that point, the longest trip that could be taken across the lakes. It was badly damaged 4 kilometres off Harbor Beach, Michigan, and had to be towed south by another ship, the *Westmount*. With the storm still raging, *Westmount*—which was also pulling another damaged ship, the *Melrose*—was forced to cut the rope. The *Minnedosa* was cut loose and consequently sunk. It went down at approximately 2 AM on October 20, off Saginaw Bay in Lake Huron. With it were lost nine sailors and 50,000 bushels of wheat. The wreck was not discovered until 1993.

Another notable loss during the storm was the *Tasmania*, which sunk off Pelee Island on October 22. It was also being towed after sustaining earlier damages. The *Bulgaria* was bringing *Tasmania* towards Cleveland, along with another ship, *Ashland*.

"The *Ashland* was lost to view of the *Bulgaria*," reported the *Buffalo News*.

> *Those on board the* Ashland *could dimly see the* Tasmania. *One moment she rode toward it on great waves; another moment she receded in the trough of the sea. On board the* Ashland, *they were keeping from being washed into the sea only by clinging to objects on deck. It was seen that the line to the* Ashland *must be cut. One of the crew made his way to the stern. With a knife he reached down and severed the line. The end of it dropped away out of sight. That was the last the crew of the* Ashland *saw of the other boat. It seemed that she sank at once.*

The wreck was discovered shortly afterwards, in shallow waters east of Pelee. In order to prevent other ships from cashing into it, the federal government ordered it blown up.

Porcupine Fire

❧◆❧

July 11, 1911
South Porcupine (Cochrane District)

GOLD WAS DISCOVERED IN the Cochrane District of northern Ontario in 1909. Prospectors George Bannerman and Tom Geddes came across gold on the south shore of Lake Porcupine while trekking through the almost completely unexplored territory north of North Bay. (The larger town of Timmins would be founded nearby in 1912.)

Gold rushes have a way of drawing people at almost unimaginable speeds, and so, within two years, a small but booming town of 3000 sprung up, named South Porcupine. (Its name refers to its position on Lake Porcupine; there is no "North Porcupine.") Indeed, things were going so well that by 1911, the town was already building its second generation of homes. Many of the "old timers" who had arrived in 1909 and built log cabins were now replacing them with proper houses. On July 1, 1911, railway service to South Porcupine was inaugurated, allowing for faster transportation of materials and people.

But at the very moment the town was seeing its biggest success, it was struck by tragedy. July had been a very dry month that year—there had been no rain at all for six weeks. A forest fire began near the town on July 11. The fire's path was later traced all the way from Lake Superior to Lake Abitibi. It burned 20 townships on its way.

South Porcupine resident James Forsyth recalled that he felt worried the morning of July 11. By 10 AM, he could see a dark, smoky cloud on the horizon, and he felt a gentle wind blowing towards the town. "I'll get a boat and go across [Lake Porcupine] to Golden City," his wife Edith said to him, packing her suitcase and taking her cocker spaniel, Peter. "It will be safer there."

After his wife left, with nothing else to do, Forsyth went to have a drink at Andy Leroux's pub with his business partner—none other than gold prospector Tom Geddes. "It looks like it will get us," remarked Geddes to the bartender. "Maybe," said Leroux. "You can never tell with a fire. It depends on the wind."

At 12:30 PM, there was no question that the fire was threatening the town. Forsyth and Geddes went to protect their company office, carrying buckets of water to douse the fire as it got closer. At that point, the wind increased. Burning branches and bark—swept up from the forest by the wind—began to rain down on South Porcupine. At 1:15 PM, Forsyth heard the fire whistle blow at the massive Dome Mine, a few kilometres outside of town.

Sixty men at the Dome Mine survived the fire by leaping into a nearby reservoir pond. But one man panicked and jumped out of the water and into the fire. His body was later found, completely burned.

At 1:25 PM, it was clear that there was no point in trying to save the company office; Forsyth ran for his life towards the lake. For the final several hundred metres, before reaching the shore, he was on his hands and knees, hardly able to breathe. Barely conscious and gasping for air, he eventually made it to Lake Porcupine. He stood in the frigid water up to his head for three hours, not sure if he would survive. He grasped onto a branch, underwater, in case the winds and waves might pull him away from shore.

The rest of South Porcupine's citizens were also heading for Porcupine Lake, clamouring for the few boats and canoes docked at the beach. Many residents had become rich during the gold rush of the past couple years and were reluctant to give up their new possessions. Several men suddenly rushed back to their houses to grab some precious item and were left for dead when they did not return. One woman was prepared to leave in style, carrying bags of luggage, furs and a caged canary. A man helped her into a boat, and then he promptly threw her belongings overboard.

Two men jumped out of their boat to save a drowning woman named Rosie, who ran the local laundry. They held on to her for two hours, entertaining her with Scottish songs. Another woman successfully gave birth while standing in the lake waiting for the fire to pass.

The *Sudbury Star* reported, "It is related that one refugee lay on his back in shallow water, with only his nose protruding above the surface in order to breathe. His nose was burned completely off by a flame which shot out over the water from the bush near the shore."

At 1:40 PM, a railway car carrying dynamite exploded near the edge of the lake. Luckily, the soft, swampy ground nearby absorbed most of the force of the explosion. Nevertheless, the blast sent tidal waves across Lake Porcupine, knocking over many of the boats and canoes of the escaping townspeople, some of whom drowned in the confusion. In Golden City, about 3 kilometres from the lake, every pane of glass in town was smashed. A crater 15 metres wide and over 4 metres deep was left behind, severing the newly laid railway track.

Golden City itself might have burned if it wasn't for a swamp in between it and South Porcupine and a previous fire that had burned out some of the surrounding forest.

Over at the West Dome Mine, (some ways from the main Dome Mine) a very different story unfolded. The mine was surrounded by fire, and there was nowhere left to run. Several people burned to death in the forest

The great forest fire of 1911 reaches the mining boom town of South Porcupine. The town was destroyed and its residents were forced to flee across Lake Porcupine.

next to the mine, in an attempt to flee the fire. Robert Weiss, the local mine boss, decided to seek shelter in the mine shaft while the fire passed over the surface. He took his wife Jennie and three-year-old daughter Ariel with him, as well as 17 other miners trapped in the area.

Weiss had been worried about fires for some time. Just one day earlier he had told a friend, "These fires have got my goat. I can't sleep at night they're a regular nightmare." The fear proved prophetic. Indeed, as any student of physics could have predicted, the fire sucked the oxygen out of the mine shaft and suffocated everyone inside. Only one miner changed his mind about the plan and returned to the surface, managing to dodge the fire and survive the ordeal.

Weiss was found with his daughter in his arms and his wife close by, all three of them dead. A huge man, weighing nearly 200 kilograms and standing nearly 2 metres tall, Weiss had to be lifted out with a block and tackle. Later, it took 14 men to carry his coffin.

In the adjacent village of Aura Lake, which was also burned, some frenzied residents attempted to steal the canoe belonging to Dayton Ostrosser, the local postmaster. Ostrosser convinced them to abandon their scheme—with the barrel of his gun. In many small villages like Aura Lake, the postmaster was the only government official and also had to play the role of police chief and mayor. The only object Ostrosser saved from the local post office was the date stamp. He used it the day after the fire to process letters and postcards that the survivors sent to their relatives. Most of the letters were written on birch bark, because all the paper had been destroyed. And because the postal bags had also burned, the mail was carried out of town in oat sacks.

Witnesses reported that blocks of ice—used to keep food cool before the invention of refrigerators—were one of the few things left standing in South Porcupine. The ice remained, somewhat melted, in icehouses that had almost completely burned away.

The fire had destroyed everything built in the town over its first three years. It even burned up the soft, peat-filled soil (known as muskeg). Indeed, after the fire, the ground level of South Porcupine had gone down half a metre! In some places, only bare bedrock remained.

Two pigs and 13 piglets were roasted alive in the fire. It was reported that some miners who had returned to survey the damages ate them.

By the end of the week, a heavy rainfall occurred, and the danger of fire was over for the summer. However, it was little consolation for the town's survivors, who had lost their friends, relatives, homes and possessions. In all, three town sites—the camps around mines—had been completely lost. When the railway track was repaired and the first train since the fire pulled out of South Porcupine, 1200 people left with it. James Forsyth left with them and never returned. Although he had lost his business, his home and all his possessions, he considered himself lucky to be alive.

Seventy-three people were reported to have died in the fire, though many believed the toll was actually much higher. Many of the miners and prospectors had been drifters who had no families to report them missing, and some had lived outside of town in the forest.

The dead were buried in the town's graveyard at Edward's Point, which became known as Deadman's Point.

Great Lakes Storm of 1913

ONE OF THE MOST SERIOUS PROBLEMS of cargo shipping in the Great Lakes has always been about getting freighters between one body of water and another.

Over time, canals were built to connect the lakes and, because the water level of each lake is different, great locks were constructed. The Soo Locks at Sault Ste. Marie ended the old portage around the rapids of St. Mary's River. Channels were established through the St. Clair and Detroit rivers, and the Welland Canal allowed the Niagara River to be bypassed entirely.

These rivers and canals were by nature less deep than the lakes themselves. Freighters had to be built with shallow hulls, which were different from ocean-going ships, in order to make it through. This practice seemed sensible when the weather was good, but throughout the early 20th century, the unstable shape of these huge freighters made many of them the victims of savage storms while navigating the deeper waters of the lakes.

The worst of these storms—a combined hurricane and blizzard—occurred in 1913. In those days, hurricanes were not yet given names, and they were an extremely rare occurrence so far inland. The 1913 storm caught Ontarians by surprise, just as it would with Hurricane Hazel in 1955, two years after hurricanes were given alternating male and female names.

November 17 was the start of four days of nonstop snowing and high winds. The United States Weather Bureau issued a telegraph to ports across the American side of the lakes warning them of the danger, but it was largely unheeded. For most shipping companies, time was simply too valuable to waste by leaving the freights in port.

Beginning over Minnesota, the storm was, like many Great Lakes storms, the result of warm, moist air from the Gulf of Mexico colliding with cold winds from the Arctic. Hunters near Sudbury reported that animals seemed to sense the danger—deer, moose and bears had deserted swamps and began to seek higher ground.

The storm surged east across Michigan to Marquette, then picked up speed around Sault Ste. Marie and entered Lake Huron. It climaxed on Sunday night, November 9, with winds of up to 150 kilometres per hour. Waves reached over 12 metres in height.

The results were tragic. On Lake Huron, the worst hit of the Great Lakes, eight ships were sunk with all hands. These included the *Isaac M. Scott* and the *Charles S. Price*, each with a load of coal and a crew of 28. A further 28 sailors were lost on board the *Hydrus,* as well as 25 from the *Argus.* The body of Emily Walker, the *Argus'* cook, was found wearing the captain's life preserver and the chief engineer's jacket—apparently gallantly offered to her, but to no avail. Three men who had survived the sinking of the *Regina* were found dead from exposure in their still-floating lifeboat.

The *James C. Carruthers,* only five months old and one of the largest freighters on the lakes, survived the storm on Lake Superior but was sunk when it followed the hurricane into Lake Huron. One man, Thomas Thompson, later thought that he had identified the body of his son, John, a crew member of the *James C. Carruther.* Identifying marks included certain missing teeth, a burn mark on one shin and initials tattooed on his left forearm. Although the corpse had lighter hair than Thompson remembered his son having, this was explained by the amount of time John had been underwater. However, Thompson was in for a surprise—John later walked in on his own wake.

On Lake Superior, the results of the storm were almost as fatal as that on Lake Huron. The winds were powerful enough to snap the 5-centimetre-thick steel mooring cables and to drag docked ships out into the lake. The *Turret Chief*'s crew found their ship dragged 160 kilometres off course before being grounded near Copper Harbour. The *L.C. Waldo* was impaled on Gull Rock on Superior's shore by 9-metre waves. Its crew survived by burning everything they could find, including parts of the ship, to keep warm until they were rescued days later. The great passenger ship *Huronic*—sister ship of the *Noronic*, which was tragically to burn in 1949—was badly damaged and grounded in Whitefish Bay.

The *William Nottingham*'s engines fought against the force of the storm for two days, until the ship ran out of coal. Its crew then began burning the cargo of grain to power the ship into Whitefish Bay. However, it ran aground on the reefs near Sandy Island. The crew sent a lifeboat with three men on board to seek help, but the force of the waves smashed the lifeboat back against the ship's hull, killing all three. The remaining crew of 15 were eventually discovered and rescued.

Knowing the danger they might face, the crew of the *Henry B. Smith* set sail in the midst of the storm, attempting to finish the season's last haul of coal. The ship was so severely destroyed that scraps of metal that had washed up on the shores of Lake Michigan were its only remains. The crew of 25 were all lost.

Another ship, *Leafield*, disappeared in Lake Superior with absolutely no trace, after being last spotted off Angus Island. No remains of the ship or its 18 crew have ever been found.

On Lake Erie, witnesses watched the steamer *Calcite* being pulverized before their eyes. Waves smashed its rigging, lights, lifeboats and windows before it eventually sunk. On the wreck of *U.S. Lightboat #82*, the words "Good-bye Nellie, the ship is breaking up fast. Williams" were found scrawled on a door. The body of Captain Hugh Williams washed up on shore a few days after the storm.

Tragedies also struck the American waters of Lake Michigan. One steamer there, *Louisiana*, was grounded near Green Bay. Its crew found their way to shore in a lifeboat but had difficulty making their way through the heavy snowdrifts that eventually covered them. To dig themselves out, they chose the shortest man in their group, swung him around and flung him repeatedly at the snowbanks. Using this method, they were eventually able to carve out a trail to a nearby farmhouse where they found shelter. The unfortunate short man survived as well, though he later wrote, "I didn't like this chilly trick too well..."

Although Canadian cities on the lakes didn't fare too badly, a number of American ports were seriously battered. Cleveland received the worst loss—all the ships in its harbour were destroyed, and the city had $5 million worth of damage.

In more recent days, the Great Lakes have become a haven for divers who enjoy exploring the historic shipwrecks that remain underwater. The wreck of the *Regina* was not discovered until 1987. Divers brought up an unusual sunken treasure—a cargo of not only intact but also drinkable and well-aged bottles of scotch and champagne. They were sold at auction in Chicago. An estimated $2 million in gold—on its way to cover the payroll of the workers building the Sault Ste. Marie docks—was also on board the *Regina*. The gold is believed to still be in Lake Erie, in a rusted safe 25 metres below the surface.

In 2000, the wreck of the 82 metre-long freighter *Wexford* was discovered in Lake Huron, between Bayfield and Grand Bend. Fisherman Don Chalmers had his line snag on something, and his fish finder showed a large object a fair distance under the surface. He later went diving at the same spot and found the huge boat in pristine condition. Beforehand, the only sign of the ship had been a plank of wood that had washed up in Goderich after the storm. It read, "I am with the boat, lashed to the wheel. —B," and was probably written by Captain Bruce Cameron.

Matheson Fire

IN THE FORESTS OF ALL PARTS of northern Canada, summer fires are a constant threat. A dry season can make the threat especially acute. Fires can be started by natural means, such as lightning strikes, or by human errors. Sparks flying from the old coal-burning train engines were once a common cause of forest fires. However, though fires remain a danger even today, in the early 20th century they could be completely devastating. They had the power to wipe whole communities off the map.

This is exactly what happened to the town of Matheson in 1916. Only five years after the deadly Porcupine Fire, another blaze began in the Cochrane District of northeastern Ontario. How it started is unclear. It could have been a spark off a train or a lightning strike, or a fire that had spread from an encampment—in those days, settlers in the north commonly used fires to clear away unwanted brush and debris. Or several of these causes together might have started the fire. In any case, a swift wind fed the flames and soon brought the fire to the town of Matheson.

The fire had moved the 300-kilometre distance from Bourkes, with a front of over 100 kilometres, to Hearst, where it widened to 250 kilometres. During this time, it swept over Matheson.

Residents of Matheson believed they were safe, because earlier that year, smaller fires had cleared out much of the forest surrounding the town. However, the fire came with such intensity that stumps, underbrush and even the ground itself burned, carrying the inferno forwards. It approached the town from two sides.

Farmer William Dowson recalled struggling to save his farm, with the help of its co-owners and workers. It soon became clear, as more and more sparks rained down overhead, that they would have to abandon the farm.

The group was able to save themselves by hiding under a soaked tarp held up by boxes. They used a tub of water to keep the tarp damp. Dowson later said that he felt he was "at the bottom of a sea of fire thousands of feet high." So much dark smoke filled the air that it completely blacked out the sun.

At one point Dowson panicked and left the shelter, feeling that he was suffocating. As soon he was out into the burning area, he realized the error he had made, but it was almost too late. He had to pass through a wall of flame but managed to find a ditch with some damp clay in it. He jumped into the clay and was able to survive the fire. His friends in the shelter also survived.

A train happened to be passing through Matheson as the fire hit the town. It had been diverted that way because the fire had burned the bridge it normally passed over. The train stopped several times to allow hundreds of hopelessly trapped townspeople to clamour into the boxcars. However, the wooden cars themselves began to burn as the train pulled out of Matheson, and the screams of people who had been clinging on to the outside could be heard as the fire singed them. The heat caused two cars to disengage, and the people inside had to struggle through the smoke and flames to find safety in the adjacent cars. Railway ties burned underneath the train, and the heat caused the tracks to warp, slowing the train's movement.

Eventually, though charred and smoking, the train made it away from the fire.

As was the case in the Porcupine Fire, many people in the area surrounding Matheson suffocated when they sought shelter in enclosed wells and root cellars. In nearby Nushka, the local priest, Wilfred Gagné, tried to shelter his parishioners in a clay hut. The force of the fire caused the roof to collapse, and the flames spread in, killing Gagné and most of the people inside. The town was later renamed Val Gagné (Gagné Valley) in his memory.

It was said that the fire was so hot that it caused shallow creeks to boil, and fish floated up to the surface, cooked.

In total, 200,000 hectares of land were burned. The army set up a temporary mortuary in Matheson, and several trainloads of doctors, nurses, and medical supplies were rushed to the district. Between 223 and 228 people in the area were officially reported as dead, but locals suspected that the real toll was much higher. Charred bodies continued to be found in isolated encampments in the forest throughout the summer and fall, and many have never been found.

The towns of Matheson, Iroquois Falls, Porquis Junction, Nushka, Kelso and Cochrane were destroyed, as well as parts of the bigger settlement of Timmins. Only three buildings in Matheson survived, all sitting on a hill. Matheson was never rebuilt—though, miraculously, none of the people living in the town itself were reported dead. The train seemed to have saved everyone.

A heavy rainstorm occurred within a week of the blaze, bringing another summer's fire season to a close.

Spanish Influenza

1918–1919
Worldwide

THE 20TH CENTURY'S GREATEST PANDEMIC—the Spanish Influenza—arrived in Ontario on October 3, 1918. Its initial outbreak was in Toronto's Grace Hospital, carried by wounded soldiers returning from Europe, and it struck half the hospital nurses by October 8. On October 16, the city ordered all dancehalls, schools and public buildings closed, but it was little use. Spanish Influenza would go on to kill 1200 people in Toronto, 8700 in Ontario, 50,000 across Canada, and between 50 and 100 million worldwide. A whopping 20 percent of the world's population contracted Spanish Influenza, and between 2.5 and 5 percent of the total population died.

Unlike other flus, the Spanish Influenza equally affected people of all ages, not just children or the elderly. Indeed, more Canadians were killed in a year by the influenza than had been killed in the previous four years of World War I. More Americans were killed by it than in World War I, World War II, the Korean War and the Vietnam War combined. Within six months of its start, the Spanish Influenza killed more people worldwide than the current AIDS epidemic has killed in 25 years.

Only a few remote parts of the world were completely spared—including an island in northern Brazil, and the Pacific islands of New Caledonia and American Samoa—because of belated travel restrictions.

The Spanish Influenza had its global beginning in Camp Funston (a military barracks in Fort Riley, Kansas) on March 4, 1918. The disease, initially affecting birds, mutated to allow it to spread to humans. It appeared soon afterwards in Brest, France, likely brought there by American soldiers. The influenza's speed of transmission proved unstoppable, especially since military propaganda initially denied its existence and later tried to downplay it. It was considered to be bad for the war effort if the general population knew that hundreds of thousands of soldiers were dying at the front lines—not just from the war but from disease as well.

The Spanish Influenza got its name because the disease was first widely reported in the Spanish press. Because Spain was neutral during World War I, its newspapers were not subject to the same propaganda restraints as other countries. The name initially caused people to think the epidemic was a Spanish phenomenon, though it did not hit Spain any worse than other parts of the world.

Formally, the disease is known as Influenza A Virus, Subtype H1N1. It spread through the air, on small droplets of water caused by coughing or sneezing. Victims had difficulty breathing and their faces turned blue from lack of oxygen. They were too weak to walk and often coughed blood. Other diseases often resulted as complications from the influenza. Death could occur only hours after the first symptoms had been spotted.

A saying at the time was, "If your eyes begin to water and your nose turns blue, if your lips begin to quiver, then you've got the Spanish Flu!"

Two young women from Woodstock shared a room at the YWCA while working in Paris, Ontario. After work one day, Claire Hunter attended an evening lecture, and her roommate went to bed. The next morning, Claire called out to her roommate to tell her that she was going downstairs for breakfast. She heard no reply and so went ahead by herself. When she finished breakfast she went back upstairs and tried to wake her roommate. "I pulled down the sheets. She was dead and cold. The doctor said she had died around two in the morning—the 'flu had got to her quick.'" The young woman had showed no previous signs of having the influenza.

The effects on the bodies of the dead were shocking. "There was so much liquid in the air spaces of their lungs that patients would have bloody fluid coming out of their noses. When they died, it would often drench the bed sheets," said U.S. Army pathologist Jeffery Taubenberger.

In the chaos of World War I, few doctors and nurses were available to tend to the sick in Ontario. Weeks after the first case in Toronto had been reported, the city was averaging 17 deaths per day. St. John's Ambulance trained a special order of nurses in the province to deal with the outbreak, called Sisters of Service, or "SOS."

"It was as if a black, sombre cloud fell over all. People closed their doors and stayed within to keep their lives," recalled Dr. Arthur E. Parks, who was a child at the time of the outbreak. "When we did go out we saw black crepe sashes on front doors, and when we heard the church bells ring at St. Alban's we knew another one had died."

When someone died of the influenza, a sash was put on their door to mark the household. A white sash indicated that a child had died, a grey one meant an adult, and a purple sash showed that a senior had died. Churches were closed, and funerals were banned to prevent passing of the virus among mourners. Indeed, there was little time and few people available to oversee funerals anyway. Most bodies were quickly cremated, and many were put into mass graves.

Towns not yet affected by the epidemic enforced strict quarantines, threatening to arrest anyone caught entering or leaving. In many places, it was uncommon to see a single person outside without a gauze mask on.

One of the ways doctors treated infected patients was by giving them infusions of blood from others who had survived the disease. This improved their immune system and raised the chances of survival to 50 percent— a huge improvement.

In Hamilton, Dr. Elizabeth Bagshaw was making over 20 house calls a day. "We had nothing to give them as injections," she recalled. "Aspirin was almost the only thing." Bagshaw later caught the flu herself, but survived it even though she was in a house filled with sick relatives and co-workers. "We were so weak that when we carried tea upstairs we didn't bother with a saucer because that would have been extra weight to carry," she said.

In the town of Ganonoque, Dr. Godfrey Bird was seeing as many as 80 to 90 patients a day at the height of the epidemic, well above his usual 23 to 26. On October 12, 1918, it was recorded that he paid 58 house calls.

At the worst part of the plague, even doctors were frightened to go near influenza patients. Therefore, many people resorted to ad hoc home remedies. A nurse at the Kodak factory in Toronto offered ill workers three drops of carbolic acid in cups of water. Others put lard and chopped onions on their chest, or used other substances such as camphor oil, turpentine or alcohol. Tying garlic around patients' necks and putting sulphur in their shoes were also tried, as was bloodletting and pumping oxygen.

Newspapers suggested helpfully (but incorrectly) that people should "avoid getting chilled, keep the hands clean, sleep and work in clean, fresh air, avoid alcoholic stimulants, don't worry—and do not kiss anyone."

By late 1918, the pandemic had subsided, and in 1919 disappeared entirely, in Ontario and around the world. It is still unclear why the disease stopped, since no successful cure or vaccine for it has ever been developed. Scientists generally speculate that the remaining population developed an immunity to the influenza or that it had mutated into a harmless form. Flus tend to mutate at an incredible rate, and this is what forces the World Health Organization and other similar groups to develop new flu vaccines twice every year.

The original Spanish Influenza virus was preserved in an Alaskan woman who died of it and whose body was frozen in permafrost. Eighty-five percent of the people in Brevig Mission, the town where she lived, died in the epidemic. Scientists were able to extract the virus from the corpse in order to study it. The virus remains—under high security—in several labs around the world, where it continues to be studied. In 2005, the genetic sequence of Spanish Influenza was finally mapped, though there is still no cure.

On average, two global pandemics occur per century—but the 20th century had only one. Because scientists fear that another influenza virus, such as the "Bird Flu," might mutate to become highly contagious and deadly among humans, the history of the Spanish Influenza remains the focus of study. To date, unfortunately, little has been learned that could be used to prevent a new disease from decimating the world's population.

Polio Epidemic

1927–1962
Worldwide

WHAT DO JONI MITCHELL, Neil Young, Donald Sutherland and Jean Chrétien all have in common? Besides being famous Canadians, all of them once had polio. Between 1927 and 1962, 50,000 Canadians contracted poliomyelitis (polio for short), and 4700 died. Others suffered permanent disabilities or disfigurations (such as the twist in Jean Chrétien's upper lip and his lack of hearing in one ear).

Known as "the Crippler," polio was a disease that mainly affected children. It entered the digestive system through the indigestion of contaminated food or water and then spread to the circulatory and nervous systems, where it caused muscle weakness and in some cases paralysis.

Symptoms often wouldn't appear for a month or longer, giving ample time for the germs to spread, usually through feces. Initially, children complained of sore muscles, tiredness, fever, headaches or vomiting—symptoms often mistaken for a normal flu.

Of those patients who developed paralytic polio—the worst form of the disease—10 percent died, and 40 percent became paralyzed or disfigured for life. Polio spread through the spinal cord and in some cases damaged the muscles that control breathing. Patients who could not breathe had to be placed in giant metallic tanks—known as "iron lungs"—in hospital wards, where the machinery would allow them to breathe. Only the patient's head was exposed, and the patient was often forced to stay inside the iron lung for months at a time.

The disease was first recorded in Germany in 1840, but it wasn't until the mid 20th century that it became an epidemic and made its appearance in Canada. It is speculated that polio's history actually dates back to early times—recorded descriptions suggest that ancient Egyptians suffered from it.

In Ontario, polio caused panic wherever it spread. It hit its height in 1953. Schools and churches were frequently closed, because it was (incorrectly) feared that germs might be left behind when someone had recently died. Children under 16—those most likely to catch the disease—were often banned from public places, and cities became eerily empty in the summer.

Ironically, children who lived in less sanitary conditions were less likely to catch the disease. It seems that repeated exposure to small amounts of the virus had immunized them. Children living in cleaner conditions had weakened immune systems, and the disease—if they caught it later—would be a shock to their system.

Barbara Bondar of Toronto, in a statement made to Canada's National Polio Survival Network, recalls surviving the disease. "Once at the hospital, I was made to curl up in a ball while fluid was taken from my spine. I was diagnosed with polio. My parents were told to be prepared to lose their daughter.

"I remember my legs hurting and the pain that seemed to come from everywhere. I was very frightened that I might die and began to make bargains with God that I would be 'good' if only the pain would go away. I wasn't able to eat or drink.

"Someone brought a bowl into my room that contained a long rubber tube sitting in ice. She inserted it through my nose into my stomach so that I could be fed for the next couple of weeks..."

Bondar was given a book to read but was too weak to hold it up. Her parents were allowed to visit her, but only if they wore white robes and masks. She was later taken to Sick Children's Hospital and Thistletown Hospital.

"My speech was nasal, and, although I didn't realize it at the time, my right facial muscles were paralyzed. That was the most difficult aspect of my experience with polio to accept."

A number of failed attempts were made to treat the disease. In Toronto in 1937, inventor Edwin Schultz tested an experimental nasal spray vaccine on 5000 children. None of them were successfully prevented from catching polio, and many lost their sense of smell. It was also thought at one point that the pesticide DDT could kill the disease. Many towns in Ontario were sprayed with DDT, before DDT itself was banned for its fatal effects.

However, it was researchers at the Connaught lab at the University of Toronto who assisted in the breakthrough that finally cured the disease. After the development of the first successful vaccine in Boston in 1953, the lab discovered a tissue culture for polio that could be kept alive and injected in very small doses into children, preventing them from catching the disease. The lab also discovered how to multiply the culture so that mass vaccinations could take place. All polio vaccines in Canada came out of the Connaught lab—and within a few years, the spread of polio in Canada was finally stopped.

Many victims of the disease in Ontario continue to live with its effects. These include "post-polio syndrome," in which victims, though fully recovered, start experiencing pain and weakness decades later. Indeed, many people who had mild cases of polio and recovered quickly only learned years afterwards that they had had the disease because of the onset of post-polio syndrome.

Elsewhere in the world, however, polio still exists. The last case in the Americas (other than a brief outbreak in Haiti in 2002) was in Peru in 1991. As of 2006, 1763 people continue to suffer from polio—mostly in Nigeria, Afghanistan, Pakistan and India. A controversial alternative vaccine used in some parts of the world—including China, Japan, Africa and the former Soviet bloc—seems to have actually caused more cases of polio than it prevented.

Heat Wave of 1936

IN CANADA, A HEAT WAVE IS DEFINED AS THREE or more consecutive days in which the temperature rises above 32°C, not including the humidity factor. Heat waves are common in Ontario, especially in the past decade, as global warming has increased temperatures. With cool, air conditioned houses and better preparedness, people are now able to handle extreme heat fairly well.

However, in 1936, at the height of the Great Depression, this was not the case. The same heat wave that contributed to the dustbowls of the Prairies caused a great number of deaths in Ontario. Many of the dead were homeless people, made destitute by the economic collapse. In poor health and with little access to shelter, they were vulnerable to the elements, as were young children and the elderly.

Air conditioners did exist in the 1930s, but they were too expensive for most people to afford, especially in a province that didn't have a reputation for blistering heat. The now-familiar whirring could be heard in a few upscale department stores, movie theatres, government offices and in the homes of the very rich.

The high temperatures that had started in June in the United States rolled into northern Ontario and Manitoba on July 7. By July 14, the entire province of Ontario was sweltering. Record temperatures were set on July 11 and 12 in Atikokan, and July 13 in Fort Frances. On all three occasions, it rose to 42.2°C. Environment Canada reported that temperatures on reflective surfaces rose as high as 65°C.

Toronto experienced its highest temperature to date when it rose to 41.1°C on July 10. The city also recorded its highest overnight low, 26.6°C, on July 11. On that day, 30 Torontonians died of heat exposure, 22 of them dying between the hours of 4 and 9 PM alone. In total, 225 people died of the heat wave in the province's capital city. In the westend suburb of Mimico, a pile of hay spontaneously combusted under the heat, eventually burning down an entire block of houses.

Between 780 and 1180 deaths across the country were blamed on the heat wave, including 600 in Ontario. Another 400 inexperienced swimmers drowned that summer, while trying to cool off. To put these numbers in perspective, only 47 Canadians were reported as dying from heat during the previous summer.

It was so hot that steel railway tracks and bridge girders were warped by the heat, and concrete sidewalks cracked and buckled. Crops were decimated as the heat dried up wells and agricultural reservoirs. Fruit was reported to have been found baked, still on the trees. With the ruin of the year's crop, food prices rose tremendously, threatening the poorest victims of the Depression with starvation. This lead the province to initiate a controversial food-based welfare system, in which the poorest quality crops were bought up and distributed to the poor.

By the end of the week, temperatures returned to normal. And, as if to mock Ontarians, the province also went on to suffer one of its coldest winters ever that year.

Thames River Flood

◆

April 26, 1937
Middlesex, Oxford and Perth Counties

THE THAMES RIVER'S TWO BRANCHES BEGIN near Mitchell and Woodstock. They converge in the city of London and flow through Chatham before reaching Lake St. Clair at Lighthouse Cove. The river—originally known as the Askunessippi—was renamed Thames in 1793 to coincide with the founding of London, Ontario. Lieutenant-Governor John Graves Simcoe hoped—in vain—to create a miniature duplicate of London, UK, complete with its famous river.

The Thames River of Ontario is noticeably smaller than its English counterpart, but it still has the possibility to cause disasters. As well as being the site of the *Queen Victoria*'s sinking in 1881, the Thames has had its share of serious floods.

Early settlers reported a number of floods, but they did not occur often enough to prevent people from building along the riverbanks. In fact, too much construction and poor agricultural practices caused soil erosion, opening up the possibility of serious flood damage.

The first well-known flood occurred in 1883, drowning 12 people. After that, new safety measures were put in place, including a series of dykes to prevent areas from becoming swamped. However, the dykes did not stop a second, much larger—although less fatal—flood from occurring half a century later.

On April 26, 1937, a dam on the Avon River in Stratford (another English-inspired town and river combination) burst, sending tremendous amounts of water into the North Thames River. An exceptionally heavy snowfall that winter, combined with a sudden rise in the temperature, caused excessive runoff, leading to the initial flood. On top of this, the area had suffered four straight days of heavy rains. The town of St. Mary's was quickly submerged, followed by London itself.

The entire Thames saw its water level rise by between 5 and 10 metres—in less than a day. Dozens of dams and dykes, built to control the river, were broken or simply overwhelmed by the surging water.

Only one drowning death was reported in direct connection to the flood of 1937. London resident Joseph Brytton drowned while successfully rescuing a family trapped by the river. His boat capsized in the heavy currents. His friend Charles Selby, who had been travelling with him, managed to swim to safety.

However, four or five others died when a passing train was hit by rising waters. The waters of the Thames weakened a portion of the tracks, partially washing out the ground underneath it. With the weight of the engine, the rail gave way completely, causing the engine, the baggage car and one coach to leave the tracks and sink into the water.

The train's fireman, Norman Aiken, was killed instantly in the crash. Its engineer, Malcolm Isbister, died three hours later of the wounds he suffered from the accident. Dr. J.H. Macdonald, who lived nearby, heard about the crash and raced there in his car to assist the survivors. However, his car was swept up by the floodwaters and he too drowned. Alyre LeBlanc—a hobo riding covertly in the baggage car—lost his life. It was reported that there might have been another vagrant on the train who also died in the crash.

The *Toronto Star* reported that some Londoners were unwilling to leave their homes, despite the rising waters.

There was Mrs. X from Winnipeg Ave. for instance. So far as human companionship was concerned she lived alone. The police knew this and when floodwaters engulfed her home they made a rescue dash. But Mrs. X would have none of their help unless they first removed her dogs…11 dogs. So they loaded 11 dogs in a boat and ferried them down street to Empress Ave. school were another cop, who must have been quite a lad, started an investigation to see if tax had been paid on all those pooches.

Among the desperate, and comical, there were also numerous acts of real heroism. "Gerald Knight and Bill Clipperton rescued a woman whose leg was encased in a heavy steel support," reported *The Star*.

While rowing her to safety a man was heard scream-ing for help. They located him clinging to a telegraph pole. Not the top of the pole, but the side, where his hold could not last long. Going to his aid the boat bumped a house, wobbled dangerously, filled with water and sank. The officers tried swimming with the woman. It was no go. They were in heavy rubber clothing. Knight, a tall man, tried to touch bottom, and found that by straightening his neck to full height he could keep his head above the flood. But that was no good either.… Like the last-minute salvation of a movie hero he then discovered a flight of steps under him. Steps that had been torn from a house. Standing on these he righted the boat; got Clipperton back aboard and saved both the lame woman and the frantic man.

The physical effects of the flooding on the area were immense. Ten thousand local residents were evacuated, and 1050 homes were flooded by the next day, leaving many homeless. Downed power lines cut off electricity to the entire area. There was tremendous damage to roads and bridges, as well as farmlands, business and houses. London estimated that in one day, the flood had caused between $3 and $10 million damage within its boundaries alone.

The worst-hit parts of London included the upscale west London suburbs of Broughdale, South London and Chelsea Green. Every highway leading to the city was submerged, and only minimal railway access remained.

A water-boiling advisory went into effect in Stratford when polluted floodwater spread into wells. Health problems due to dehydration were also reported in the area.

However, some business owners had made preparations. "Anticipating the collapse of the Thames Street Bridge in Ingersoll, a South Side baker made extra deliveries to the North side Tuesday night," the *Globe and Mail* reported. "In the middle of the night the bridge was swept away and his competitors were cut off from their customers in the morning."

That spring, scores of other towns on different rivers suffered serious flooding, including Tillsonburg, Aylmer, Hamilton, Brantford, Dunnville, Kitchener and St. Thomas. Although the devastation was not as great as along the Thames, disasters did occur. *The Globe* reported that 48,000 eggs in electric incubators were spoiled when a chick hatchery near Dunnville lost power due to flooding.

In the end, the flood of 1937 caused the government to dramatically revise the measures it took to control spring runoffs. Larger and stronger dykes and dams were constructed, and flood-warning systems were improved.

Honeymoon Bridge Collapse

TODAY'S TOURISTS WOULD PROBABLY APPRECIATE a bridge that crosses the Niagara River right below Niagara Falls. Such a bridge did once exist. The appropriately nicknamed "Honeymoon Bridge" (officially known as the Upper Steel Arch Bridge) was built in 1888. It offered tourists a chance to stop above the river and get a direct, frontal view of the Horseshoe Falls. Not surprisingly, the view features prominently in many turn-of-the century postcards and wedding photos.

The Honeymoon Bridge started to collapse between January 26 and 28, 1938, on the year of its 50th anniversary.

That month, the Niagara River had seen one of the worst buildups of ice in its history. Gales travelling over Lake Erie had pushed huge ice masses down the river, but they all came to a halt at the Honeymoon Bridge. This caused other immediate problems—the *Maid of the Mist* steamer, which brought tourists to the bottom of the Falls was damaged, pushed off its winter dry-dock by ice. There were also fears about the safety of the hydroelectric stations.

An ice jam had formed around the pillars of the Honeymoon Bridge, and there was concern about the effects the rushing river might have if the ice was not broken up. On January 26 the bridge was closed while workers tried to chip away the ice. Joined together by ropes, the team also placed 30-centimetre timbers under the bridge to reinforce the steel that was now starting to buckle.

Once the ultimate site for wedding photography, Niagara Falls' "Honeymoon Bridge" was destroyed by an ice buildup in the winter of 1938.

By January 27 the bridge had a 15-centimetre crack down its centre, and the girders under the southern arch of the bridge were beginning to seriously buckle out of line. Some ominous rumbling was heard from below, and the Canadian and U.S. governments decided to remove customs staff from the bridge area for their own safety. At this point in time, ice was piled as high as 20 metres above the water level of the river—more than one-third of the way up the bridge.

Suddenly, at 10:10 AM on January 28, a customs official reported that "the ice rose 25 feet within 10 minutes." The steel girders began to snap. However, it wasn't until the afternoon that matters came to a head. It took only eight seconds for the bridge to pull away from its moorings and drop 30 metres onto the ice jam below. Onlookers heard a loud ripping noise.

The bridge, valued at $2 million the day before, was now worth only $30,000 in salvageable scrap.

"I came down to see the wrecked tourist bridge. It is a pathetic spectacle, like a child's toy construction set that somebody had stepped on in the dark," wrote *Toronto Star* journalist Gregory Clark. "That pitiable junk streak across the ice is a mere trifle amidst the awful masses of crevassed and heaved and riven ice, foul with the mud of Lake Erie, frosted with a little new fallen snow."

Luckily, no one had been killed or injured in the collapse. And indeed, even the sightseeing industry bounced back quickly. With visitors arriving to see the remains of the bridge, the winter of 1938 became the Falls' busiest tourist season to date. Newspapers reported that 10,000 Torontonians had clamoured to stare into the icy precipice the weekend of the collapse. Work began immediately to build a new bridge, the Rainbow Bridge, which opened in 1941 and still stands today.

Great Lakes Storm of 1940

THE GREAT LAKES STORM OF 1940—also known as the "Armistice Day Storm"—took place during the night of November 11. No less than 12 ships were foundered on Lake Huron, and three were sunk. A total of 69 sailors died.

The 120 kilometre per hour winds and 10-metre high waves blew the water out of Michigan's Saginaw River and into Lake Huron. The Canadian ship *Anna C. Minch* was broken in two on the lake. It sunk, with so survivors. The American *William B. Davock* was similarly lost.

A number of Canadian sailors also faced disaster in the American waters in Lake Michigan. The *Novadoc,* on route from Chicago to Montréal, was wrecked on a reef near Pentwater, Michigan. It had received no warning of the storm and faced the winds head-on. Despite some manoeuvres by the captain to escape the storm, a wave smashed through the glass of the wheelhouse at 7 PM, and the ship hit land.

Two members of the crew died, and the rest were stranded on the reef for two days. All the lifeboats had been washed away, so they had no hope of escape. Luckily, the reef was 50 metres from the mainland, and when the crew waved a sheet they were spotted by locals. A crowd of hundreds quickly formed and watched helplessly. The shipwrecked crew tried to float a rope to the mainland but found it an impossible task.

"We kept sending up rockets to let the people on shore know that we were still alive," *Novadoc* sailor Lloyd H. Belcher of Mississauga told the *Globe and Mail*.

> *As darkness came on for the second night we saw that we had no chance of being rescued that day so we all sat around hoping for the best. By this time we were cold and getting quite hungry as we had nothing to eat for two days. The mate then found a pail and made a little fire in it to warm us up a bit. We broke up the chairs and furniture for wood and when that was all gone we started on the walls—we had a little axe with us so we broke up the walls with it. On shore they kept a fire going all the time to try to encourage us and to let us know there was nothing to do but wait until help arrived.*

The survivors were forced to wait on the reef until they were rescued under dangerous conditions by the tugboat, *Three Brothers*. The crew of the *Three Brothers* were later given an award for their bravery.

Windsor Tornado

---◆---

June 17, 1946
Essex County, near Windsor

THE 1946 TORNADO BEGAN on the American side of the Detroit River, near Melvindale, a town north of Detroit. Near the river, within sight of Windsor, it hit an abandoned armaments warehouse, still containing shells left over from World War II. Live bombs were blown into the river, prompting the government to issue warnings to local boaters.

An American military aircraft was swept off the ground from an airport and carried across the river, where it smashed into a Windsor house, killing those inside.

After passing through the River Rouge area of Detroit, the tornado crossed over to the Canadian side of the border. It then became a "waterspout" (a tornado made out of water) while crossing the river, an extremely rare phenomenon. Striking land just west of Windsor at 7 PM, it raced through the Seven-Mile Road, Farnham, Ojibway and Sandwich West areas.

The most remarkable thing about tornados is their speed. In Ontario, the "Windsor Tornado" covered a distance of between 40 and 50 kilometres, leaving a path of destruction 90 metres wide. All of this occurred in less than 10 minutes. In all, the tornado averaged a speed of nearly 650 kilometres per hour.

The situation near Windsor was made worse by two days of solid rain that proceeded the tornado. It was followed by yet another two days of precipitation, eventually sinking Highway 2 under half a metre of water and cutting off Essex County from the rest of the province.

A reporter from the *Globe and Mail* described the devastation. He observed "dead chickens everywhere, wood houses lay in piles like kindling, a little boy had his clothing whipped off of him, walked around nude crying for his mother."

The town of Ojibway was the worst hit. Many of the houses there were built with flimsy wood frames, allowing them to be easily picked up by the powerful winds of the tornado. One house, belonging to the Jones family, was reportedly pulled off its foundations, rolling over a number of times. Mrs. Jones was killed, Mr. Jones critically injured and three out of the family's five children were killed; the remaining two were seriously hurt.

Across the street, the Paré family survived, huddled together and praying, though the roof of their home was taken off and all its windows smashed.

"Outside I found a hockey skate embedded in one of the walls [of the Paré house]. It belonged to one of the Jones' children," noted *The Globe*'s reporter.

"I heard a terrific, whirring noise and I saw the thing coming at about 50 miles-an-hour," William Laboie told *The Globe*. "I warned the folks in the house and we ran to the woods about a quarter-mile away. By the time we got there the houses behind us were gone—just as quick as that."

"We saw the house lifted from its foundation," said Mrs. Perry, who watched the scene from her window. "It just came rolling, and rolling, and rolling along. I saw the house go up in the air and I saw the bodies being carried away by the wind. I don't know what became of them."

Another nearby resident, Roy Smith, watched helplessly as his house was swept away with his wife and infant child inside. The child died and his wife was seriously injured in the incident.

Dooley Cohane, an off-duty American police officer driving on the Canadian side of the border, attempted to outrace the tornado in his pickup truck. He saw lines of hydro poles being ripped out of the ground behind him, giving off flashes of light as the live wires snapped. He also saw rows of houses destroyed, and the debris smacked against the back of his truck. Luckily, the tornado changed directions and he managed to escape.

When the tornado hit the Michigan Central Railway marshalling yards outside of Windsor, entire box cars were swept up into the air and then dropped to the ground.

The entire Windsor area remained without power, the tornado having torn out the hydro lines. Telephone and telegraph service to Windsor was also knocked out for about 17 hours. Ironically, the brightest spot in the area was the Windsor-Detroit tunnel. The tunnel had its own generator, so the lights remained on underground.

After devastating the outskirts of Windsor, the tornado veered south, tearing up entire fields of corn, tomatoes and tobacco. Residents found themselves pelted with vegetables and other debris thrown up by the winds. Within minutes, the tornado reached Lake Erie and dissipated.

In Ontario, 14 people were killed and another 155 injured. There were two deaths and 34 injuries on the American side.

The most shocking death came in rural Essex county when a man was thrown against the trunk of a big tree with such force that his body became imbedded there. The man and tree were buried together.

Hurricane Hazel

October 15–16, 1954
Toronto and York County

NO ONE EXPECTED IT. WHO COULD BLAME THEM? The thought of a hurricane coming as far inland as Ontario would have seemed ridiculous before October 15, 1954. Not so after that. The memory of Hurricane Hazel is etched firmly into the memory of anyone old enough to have lived through it, as well as into the minds of many younger people who have heard the tales. Hazel became Toronto's storm of the century.

The hurricane began far away, off the coast of West Africa. By the time it reached the Caribbean, it was clear that this was no minor storm. It tore through Grenada and Carriacou, then the Dominican Republic and Haiti, before reaching the Carolinas. It killed 1000 Haitians— a fact often overlooked by Ontario residents, who suffered much less by comparison. Carolinians found palm fronds as well as cookware marked "Made in Haiti" washed up on their beaches. Hazel destroyed all but two of the 275 homes in Garden City, South Carolina. At its peak, the hurricane reached a width of nearly 200 kilometres, with surrounding gales of more than 300 kilometres per hour. It killed some 95 people in the U.S., before reaching an unsuspecting southern Ontario.

Ontarians weren't all that worried about the storm. Aside from there being no history of hurricanes in the province, the weather reports suggested that Hazel would break up over the Allegheny Mountains. Everyone figured the day would be business as usual.

At 9:30 PM on October 15, the forecast was reassuring. "The intensity of this storm has decreased to the point where it should no longer be classified as a hurricane," a radio report said. "This weakening storm will continue northward, passing just east of Toronto before midnight. The main rainfall associated with it should end shortly thereafter, with occasional light rain occurring throughout the night."

Weather predictions aren't always right—sometimes with deadly consequences. The storm hit the west end of Toronto with full hurricane force at 11 PM. It collided with a cold air front, causing more rain. The city had already seen three straight days of downpour leading up to that time. In total, 23 centimetres of rain had fallen on Toronto in a span of 48 hours.

Virtually every body of water in the Toronto area overflowed—including the Humber River, the Don River, the Credit River, Highland Creek, Etobicoke Creek and Sixteen Mile Creek. Flooding in the low-lying areas around the Humber were especially deadly, with 36 people being killed as their houses were washed into the river.

Of that number, 32 were residents of Raymore Drive, a street right at the riverbank that was entirely washed out. Many of the houses were swept downstream and pulverized beyond recognition.

Annie and Joe Ward, who lived on Raymore Drive, narrowly managed to escape by climbing into their attic as their home crumbled under them. With only a screwdriver, they were able to break through the ceiling and climb out onto the roof and from there onto another house that was more securely positioned. The couple's wire-haired terrier, Lassie, who they had left for dead, was miraculously found alive later.

The water surged much faster than it could be controlled. One man was making a call from a payphone to

Search efforts take place along the Don River the day after Hurricane Hazel hit.

say he would be arriving home late, when he saw an entire parking lot of cars being swept into the water. Another man, Gerald Elliot, was driving across the bridge over the Humber at the exact moment that both banks of the river collapsed beneath him. Firefighters tried to rescue him by throwing him a hose, which he tied around his waist. Unfortunately, the hose broke, and Elliot was carried downstream. He survived only by holding onto a tree branch for four hours, at which point he was rescued by boat.

While trying to rescue some youths from the river, four firefighters on board a fire truck were all swept in by the current. A fifth firefighter held onto a branch and was almost rescued by police who had formed a human chain to the river, but a wave washed him to his death.

Another human chain was formed to rescue the occupants of the fire truck, which was wedged further down. But it too fell short, and the truck flipped over, killing all those aboard.

Nancy Thorpe, a four-month-old baby from Long Branch, became a symbol of the devastation caused by Hazel. Her parents had handed her to a firefighter to take her to higher ground. When the firefighter returned to the family's home, the house was gone, and Nancy's parents were presumed drowned in Etobicoke Creek. Nancy was passed from person to person, boat to boat, and was even balanced on the roofs of submerged houses, before being brought to St. Joseph's Hospital. A few days later, her grandparents claimed her.

Farther north in Woodbridge, 20 people were killed when an earthen dam broke, submerging a trailer park. Most of its residents were caught asleep. One Woodbridge man spent the entire night rescuing cats and dogs as they floated by his porch. By morning, he had 27 cats and 14 dogs in his home.

Still farther up into York County, the rising water broke the massive dykes surrounding the Holland Marsh, a large farming area built below sea level. Entire communities became submerged in the flooding. The de Peuter family, who lived in the area, nailed their back door shut as the waters rose. Their efforts kept the house dry, but it unexpectedly broke away from its foundations and began to float. The lights went out when the hydro cable broke— the last thing mooring the house in place—and the family found their home sailing across the marsh, occasionally banging into other buildings. One of the children reportedly became seasick as a result. Eventually the house became lodged in mounds of floating carrots. Rescuers were then able to bring the family to safety by canoe.

In total, Hurricane Hazel knocked away 20 bridges, and 4000 families were left homeless.

Sinking of the *Edmund Fitzgerald*

━━━━━━━━━━━━ ❧◆❧ ━━━━━━━━━━━━

November 10, 1975
Lake Superior

THE EDMUND FITZGERALD WAS BUILT TO DOMINATE the shipping industry. Its name recalls the heyday of the great industrial cities of the northern Great Lakes. These places, on both sides of the border—such as Thunder Bay, Sault Ste. Marie, Wilmette, St. Ignace, Duluth, Green Bay, Milwaukee and Traverse City—were often based around single industries. The industrial "rust belt" running across Ontario and the midwestern U.S. was in steep decline by 1975. But the sheer size of the region's factories, loading docks—and ships—continues to amaze visitors.

Laid down in 1958, the *Edmund Fitzgerald* was the biggest freighter on the Great Lakes until 1972, when it was surpassed by the even larger *Stuart J. Cort*. It was designed to haul vast, heavy cargoes of ore between ports. The freighter's construction changed the local shipping industry, which until then had relied on much smaller ships that worked in larger numbers.

The *Edmund Fitzgerald* was 222 metres long and weighed 13,632 tonnes (40,000 tonnes when fully loaded)—only 47 metres shorter than the *Titanic*. It was owned by the Northwestern Mutual Life Insurance Company of Milwaukee and named after its Chairman, Edmund Fitzgerald

Bad luck seemed to have fallen onto the boat from its beginning. Fitzgerald's wife was invited to christen the boat with the traditional smashing of a champagne bottle over its bow. The bottle did not break immediately, a notoriously bad omen among sailors, and it took her three swings to get it done. In addition, one of the onlookers at the ceremony suffered a heart attack, and when the ship was launched shortly afterwards, it hit a dock, damaging it slightly. In fact, the *Edmund Fitzgerald*—affectionately known as "Fitz"—went on to suffer five collisions by 1975.

In November 1975, the *Edmund Fitzgerald* was on its last voyage of the season, travelling alongside the *Arthur M. Anderson*, between Superior, Wisconsin and Detroit (Gordon Lightfoot's famous song incorrectly claims that it was heading for Cleveland). The ship's final destination was the hellishly dreary Zug Island—a vast concrete island in Detroit dedicated to steel production. (The island is now partly abandoned and featured prominently in the barren backdrops of the movie *Robocop*.)

The ship had a full load of taconite ore pellets, which were to be melted down to extract the iron. Taconite was loaded on and off the freighters by giant, specially built machines known as Huletts, which were once a feature of virtually every Great Lakes city.

The *Edmund Fitzgerald*'s captain had opted to take a route just south of the Canadian border, in hopes of avoiding the squall that had been predicted. However, at 7 PM on November 10, the ship suddenly foundered 30 kilometres south of Whitefish Bay.

Canadian-born Captain Ernest M. McSorley was set to retire within days, after a lifetime of working on lake and ocean freighters. He radioed that the storm was "the worst I've ever seen" and reported that water was beginning to seep into the hull of the ship. Two ballet pumps were at work clearing water out of the ship, but the *Edmund Fitzgerald*'s radar had been knocked out, leaving it blinded.

The situation soon got worse. The storm was producing 8-metre waves travelling 50 knots an hour. The *Arthur*

The *Edmund Fitzgerald*—the largest ship ever on the Great Lakes, when it was built—sank with all hands in a Lake Superior squall.

❧❦❧

M. Anderson radioed the *Edmund Fitzgerald* to notify it that they had just been hit by two "rogue waves" large enough to be picked up on radar. McSorley's famous response was "We are holding our own." These were his last known words.

By 7:10 PM, the *Arthur M. Anderson* could not even pick up the *Edmund Fitzgerald* on its radar. The ship was simply gone. The *Arthur M. Anderson* searched for survivors, along with the nearby freighters *William Clay Ford* and *Hilda Marjanne*. By 8:32 PM, contact was made with the coast guard, but by this time it was far too late. No survivors were found, only lifejackets and small amounts of floating debris. All 29 crew members died.

The *Edmund Fitzgerald* continues to lie where it sank, just on the Canadian side of the border, 162 metres below the surface. It hit the bottom of Lake Superior with such force that the ship came to rest on bedrock, burying itself 8 metres under the clay. Only one body has been discovered—the rest are assumed to be buried in the clay or under the wreckage.

At some point, the *Edmund Fitzgerald* broke into two pieces. The stern piece of the ship came to a rest upside down. It is speculated that this may be because the ship was actually longer than the depth of the lake. One end may have hit the bottom, and the force may have split the freighter in two. Stood on its end, the ship would have been nearly two and a half times as tall as the Parliament buildings' Peace Tower in Ottawa, which is 92 metres.

Because there were no survivors, no one can say exactly why the *Edmund Fitzgerald* sank. Since 1975, it has been the topic of much speculation and heated debate. Dozens of books and scientific studies have been written on the subject, but there is still no agreement among experts.

Many questions remain. Why, for instance, had no other freighters been sunk or even damaged in the storm? Indeed, Lake Michigan had been hit harder that night than Lake Superior. Was the ship in poor repair, its riveting and hull worn down from years of heavy cargo? Had McSorley been careless with safety on what was to be the last voyage of his career?

The ship was equipped with the most modern safety and communications tools of the time, but it did not have depth-finding equipment—a fact that may have been fatal. The U.S. Coast Guard has speculated that the ship may have run aground on the deadly Six Fathoms Shoal, between Caribou and Michipicoten Islands. They also point out that faulty hatch covers and a lack of watertight cargo bulkheads may have been a problem.

A more recent investigation by the TV show *Discovery Channel* concluded that the three "rogue waves" were alone to blame. The third wave had hit just after the ship's final radio communication.

The ship is sunk too deep to be accessible to divers. However, it was visited by submarines, including one launched by French explorer Jacques Cousteau's ship *Calypso*. Photographs have been taken and the ship's bell was raised for display in 1995. It is now at the Great Lakes Shipwreck Museum in Michigan.

In the category of popularity, the indisputable king of Great Lakes shipwrecks is the *Edmund Fitzgerald*. Although it resulted in far fewer deaths than other shipping disasters in the lakes, it was one of the biggest ships to go down.

One year after the sinking, the ship was immortalized in Lightfoot's famous ballad, "The Wreck of the *Edmund Fitzgerald*." Lightfoot, a native of Orillia, Ontario, had been inspired by a newspaper article he read about the shipwreck. His song established the *Edmund Fitzgerald* as a kind of Canadian icon, even though it was an American ship heading between American ports—and only pushed into Canadian waters by the gale that was to sink it.

As Lightfoot's song recalls, the Mariners' Church of Detroit—commonly known as the Maritime Sailors' Cathedral—rang its bell 29 times, in memory of each sailor lost. The church is the traditional place that sailors from both sides of the Great Lakes come to pray for good weather and to remember lost comrades. The bell still rings 29 times each November 10. And every March, when the ice thaws, the church's priest blesses the fleet as the ships head through the locks at Detroit.

Barrie Tornado

May 31, 1985
Barrie, as well as Simcoe and Dufferin Counties

SOUTHERN ONTARIO HAS A REPUTATION as a hot spot for tornadoes. Small tornadoes appear every year in the province, particularly in Grey and Simcoe counties, as well as in the Windsor area. The province's worst tornado hit on May 31, 1985, resulting in 13 deaths—nine in Barrie, two in Tottenham and two in Grand Valley. The tornado became known as the "Barrie Tornado."

In 1985, Barrie was a small city of 40,000, but many new houses were going up in its suburbs. The tornado touched down at the Barrie Racetrack, completely obliterating it. Transport trucks were flung around into nearby fields, and even the grass was ripped out of the ground. Simcoe Centre MPP Earl Rowe Jr.—whose family owned 80 percent of the racetrack—reported that the horses were miraculously saved from death. The walls of their barn blew away, but the roof dropped and landed on its foundations, protecting the horses from the wind. The horses' trainers were able to lead them to safety moments before the roof crumpled.

After hitting the racetrack, the tornado moved through a suburban area, cutting a path seven blocks wide. It destroyed a gas company warehouse and four factories before heading out over Lake Simcoe. It touched down again in Allandale Heights, an area of expensive new homes known as "Mortgage Hill," and flattened 100 houses there in 15 minutes. A young boy was killed there when he was thrown off his bicycle by the force of the wind and hurled headfirst into a hydro pole.

Residents of Barrie reported seeing clouds of black dust hanging over the horizon. Rescuers said they could hear phones ringing in demolished houses, as people tried to check on relatives.

Al Elliott and his two sons were sitting in the cab of a pickup truck when it was lifted off the ground and somersaulted three times in the air before hitting a tree. All three survived.

A German tourist driving between Barrie and Toronto saw a truck turned over in the middle of the road and thought there had been an accident, "but then a woman in the car beside us rolled down the window and started screaming, 'Look at the factory, look at the factory!' I didn't understand. I couldn't see any factory. But then I realised the whole factory had collapsed. It was flattened."

The tornado moved on to Tottenham, where it destroyed 50 homes, and then continued to Grand Valley. An entire street there was levelled, including the public library, town hall, community centre and medical centre. One man was killed after being sucked out the window of his pickup truck by the winds. In all, 50 residents of Grand Valley were trapped under rubble—amazingly, most of them were dug out alive.

"It got so black and I said, the last time I saw the sky like that was when I was a kid and saw a tornado," recalled Dr. Donald Mulder, Grand Valley's only physician. "I turned my back to the window, and the roof went off and the ceiling came down."

Sixty animals were killed at the home of one couple who had a reputation of taking in every stray cat, dog, rabbit or chicken.

Donato Derisnoto of Tecumseth township had his home's roof torn off by the tornado. His fridge was hurled across the kitchen and pinned him to the wall. However, when he saw a wall collapse on his wife, he managed to find the strength to push the fridge aside and lift the wall off her.

In Shelbourne, the Skyline Restaurant was demolished. The family who owned it were in their car nearby, and they reported being lifted over a metre off the ground, before being dropped down unharmed. In Orangeville, more houses and a shopping plaza were flattened. A blind man, who had built his house over a course of 20 years, found it completely eliminated in 30 seconds.

The tornado left 1000 people homeless and knocked out power to 20,000 houses. In addition to the human casualties, it caused tremendous economic damage—costing Barrie 400 jobs, at the racetrack and at a number of factories that were destroyed.

Winisk River Flood

May 16, 1986
Winisk (Kenora District)

ON MAY 16, 1986, the village of Winisk (named after the Cree word for "groundhog") was wiped out of existence by the river of the same name.

The tiny Cree community on the edge of Hudson Bay was taken by surprise in the spring of 1986 when a log jam blocked the Winisk River. This forced the river, swollen by huge amounts of melted snow and ice, to be rerouted directly through the centre of town. The flood occurred so quickly that torrential waters injured a number of villagers and resulted in floating debris. Two people were killed: a 76-year-old man who drowned and a woman who was crushed under ice blocks.

"A [telephone] pole was knocked down by a huge wave of ice and the canoe was smashed into two pieces," band member Mike Hunter told the *Globe and Mail*. "The children escaped by jumping on to an iceberg, but the mother went under a block of ice."

"This flood was one of the fastest we ever had," Chief George Hunter told *The Globe*. "It just rushed into our village in seconds. There was no way anyone could prepare for it or take along any items for use later on. All of our personal belongings, our traditional food of caribou and geese are gone. We don't have anything left. There is nothing there (in the village), just icebergs. It's a disaster up here."

All but two buildings in Winisk were washed into Hudson Bay, never to be seen again.

Rescue efforts were woefully slow. The village was far from the nearest road, leaving a helicopter landing pad as the only escape route. The flood forced many to wait for days in their canoes, while the government gradually flew them to the helicopter pad and from there to safety. "Once the first helicopter landed at Winisk Airport, I got in…and we headed out to pick up the people on the ridge," the helicopter pilot told Environment Canada.

> *Since the fog had settled in over the entire area I had to go by memory finding the ridge again, as we had about 100 to 200 yards forward visibility and 50 foot ceiling. We found the ridge and began the airlift of people, commencing with kids and one or two mothers. In all, I made eight trips back and forth…. The pick-ups in the village were tricky. I assisted people, one by one, once they had climbed over jumbled ice chunks and crushed ice and fast-flowing water, until they were within arm's reach of the helicopter skid.*

In the end, 111 were evacuated, while 18 chose to stay in the area. Those who left were transported to the village of Attawapiskat, where they spent the next year in tents.

An inquest was later held into the government's response to the tragedy. It concluded that the Department of Indian and Northern Affairs had failed to properly monitor the conditions of the river, that it did not have any plans for emergency transportation and that it had not given Winisk's residents enough opportunity to communicate their concerns about the rising waters.

"A lot of the houses were sitting on top of ice and, when the ice melts, the houses will collapse because there are no foundations," said Attawapiskat Chief Fred Wesley as he toured the destroyed village with René Fontaine, Minister of Northern Development. "One house was sitting on a block of ice 10 feet high. The people can't go back—there's nothing to go back to."

Others were angry that the town had not been moved earlier, since it was known to be located in a dangerous flood plain. Seasonal flooding was common, and there had been serious floods in 1953 and 1967. Winisk's residents had been wanting to move for 30 years.

"Our village was located on a flood zone and was not suitable for any kind of community development," said George Hunter. "We had a community plan for an 18-mile upstream site, but we always ran into funding problems. I think it's a shame that the government will finally move after I lost 2 people in the flood."

Winisk was more of a meeting place than a town. Much of its population actually lived farther inland but relied on it as a place to shop and trade items. The town had been founded in 1820 by the Hudson's Bay Company and had been the site of a Hudson's Bay trading post and Catholic mission.

Unfortunately, the survivors of the flood were unable to rebuild their community, because the site of Winisk was declared unsafe for construction. Instead, they were resettled into a new village, Peawanuk, located 30 kilometres inland, on higher ground. A total of 300 people now live in Peawanuk.

Kirkland Lake Mine Collapse

MINERS KNOW AND FEAR THE DANGERS OF ROCK BURSTS. The phenomenon occurs in exceptionally deep mines, where incredible pressure is put on certain rocks because of the shaft's structure. Explosions of tremendous force can occur as a result of rocks cracking and disintegrating under the pressure. These explosions occur naturally, rather like earthquakes. For the past century, geologists and mining engineers have worked to prevent rock bursts around mines but have had limited success.

On November 26, 1993, two spontaneous rock bursts occurred 2.5 kilometres under Kirkland Lake Mine. The mine shaft, owned by Lac Minerals Inc., was the deepest in Canada at the time.

With the help of rescue teams working 24 hours a day, 20 miners were able to escape, with only two of them suffering injures. However, two other miners, Robert Sheldon and Leonce Verrier, remained trapped in the shaft.

Rescuers found the going exceedingly difficult. The shaft collapsed around them several times, and a side shaft that they piled rock into as they redug the mine often became filled with debris. At one point, the entire machine that they used to burrow into the mine to remove the debris fell into a hole that had opened in the shaft.

It soon became clear that the situation was hopeless for the two men trapped in the mine; the rescue effort was to become a body recovery. It was not until three months later that rescuers reached the area that the miners were last reported in. Two bodies were recovered, both had been crushed under tonnes of rocks and debris.

The Ice Storm

January 1998
Eastern Ontario

SOME PEOPLE WILL GO TO EXTREMES TO GET that essential morning pick-me-up. In January 1998, it had become so cold in Limoges, Ontario, that a M. Larocque was reported to have been making coffee with a blowtorch.

That month, eastern Ontario, Québec and northern New York suffered their worst winter weather of the 20th century. Although there have been many "ice storms" in Ontario, the name "The Ice Storm" has come to symbolize those weeks of chaos and desperation.

Newspaper photographs showed downed hydro towers and flattened forests crushed by the weight of tonnes of ice. In all, 3000 kilometres of hydro lines were destroyed, including 1000 hydro pylons and 35,000 poles that collapsed. Power was cut off to millions of people, from Kingston to New Brunswick. A total of 230,000 people were without power in Ontario, some for up to 32 days. Most of the city of Montréal was briefly in the dark.

The ice storm began when a warm mass of moist air from the Pacific moved across North America and came to rest on top of a colder system in the St. Lawrence valley. It rained for several days, but because the temperature was much colder at ground level, the rain immediately turned to ice, between 7 and 11 centimetres thick.

The power even went out in Ottawa, where some people took the situation as an opportunity to devise their own alternatives. Dale Morland, an electrical engineer, determined that the only parts of his furnace that required electricity were the gas valve and the fan. He was able to rewire the valve so that the battery from his son's robot toy could power it. As for the fan, using old bicycle parts and ply-wood, he constructed a stationary bicycle that could be used as a generator. Morland said that getting the furnace running again increased the house temperature from 15 to 20°C —though it felt a lot hotter for those pedalling the bicycle generator!

In Alexandria, the local animal hospital was over-whelmed with pets that had been abandoned as their own-ers fled for warmer ground. With the Brockville, Ottawa and Vankleek Hill SPCAs shut down and the Cornwall one filling quickly, the hospital became home to many of the canine and feline victims of the storm. It took five days before a generator could finally be found for the hospital.

When the army was called in, soldiers went from house to house checking for signs of life. Many abandoned pets were found, including nine dogs that had been left at one home with nothing to eat. The dogs had tried to catch a porcupine—with predictable results. The animal hospital staff spent an evening pulling out quills.

The stress of spending a week isolated with dozens of frightened animals in a dark, cold building was a stressful one for hospital owner Janet Lalonde. At one point, her cat—unfamiliar with candles—caught on fire and came close to burning down the building.

Brockville's tiny CFJR radio station was one of the few that continued to broadcast throughout the storm—most other stations had their towers destroyed by the ice. CFJR quickly became the focus for residents wanting to learn about the state of relief efforts, and for the police and mili-tary, who were trying to communicate the latest news. The station even received calls from U.S. state troopers, since its broadcast range covered parts of northern New York state.

Radio host Bruce Wylie—who later won the Broad-caster of the Year award from the Ontario Broadcasters' Association for his work on the ice storm—said that CFJR was getting 50 calls an hour on each of its 10 lines. The sheer quantity of work Wylie did during the storm was remarkable—he was consistently on air for 12 to 14 hours a day, without including a single break, song or advertisement.

Oakley and Dorothy Bush, from just outside of Alexandria, recalled chipping through ice that was over 5 centimetres thick, just to get their barn door open. The horses inside had been trapped in the dark for days and had to be turned out onto a field that had become more like a hockey rink. The farmers had to hold up the smaller horses in order to stop them from flipping over.

The weather wasn't the only thing victims of the ice storm had to worry about. Looting and robbery were also major concerns—especially when the target was a generator. The Bushes credited their husky-retriever Zak with scaring away a potential thief, who had quietly driven on to their property and pulled up beside the generator.

Tensions also ran high within households, with family members holed up in close quarters. Oakley Bush was quoted in the book *Stories from the Ice Storm,* saying: "Someone on our battery-powered radio advised, 'If your marriage can survive this ice storm, it can last forever.' I agree."

Janet Lalonde of the animal hospital said, "The stress the crisis created is beyond anything one could imagine. There was little room for patience, and tempers were extremely short. Yet daily I heard how people were helping each other to remarkable degrees. I think the storm will have created a lot of divorces and a lot of babies!"

Hilda Benton of Cornwall got a surprise from her husband during the storm. After the power went down, she was going through her freezer and throwing out damaged items when she suddenly found a dead blue jay staring at her. Her husband had neglected to tell her that he had found the dead bird earlier that year and tossed it in the freezer with the idea of using it as a model for woodcarving.

Some 25 deaths were blamed on the storm: people who chose to stick it out in their homes without electricity and froze; those who died from carbon monoxide poisoning, because ice had jammed their chimneys; those who died in electrical fires, and those who had heart attacks while trying to dig out of their houses. At least one person was killed by falling ice.

About 100,000 people survived the storm by heading into temporary shelters, and 11,000 troops were called up to aid in the rescue effort—the largest deployment of Canadian forces since the Korean War.

Highways and railways were rendered impassible by ice. In Québec, two stranded CN diesel engines were converted into generators and used to power towns.

Livestock farmers were also badly hit—their animals needed constant heat. One Ontario farmer found 13 of his dairy cows electrocuted by a live wire broken by the weight of the ice. In all, 10 million litres of milk was dumped because it could not be kept at proper temperatures.

Some people found the ice storm to be an exciting adventure at the beginning, but by the end, the extent of the property damages began to sink in. Many returned to houses destroyed by pipes that had leaked and frozen, or homes filled with rotting food, infested by mice and other animals, and with furniture and other items still frozen rock solid.

The following spring was noted for having the worst maple syrup harvest on record, since many of the trees had simply been snapped apart.

The ice storm caused $3 billion in damages, and insurance payouts totaled $1.44 billion—three times higher than those for 1991's Calgary hailstorm, which held the previous Canadian record.

SARS Epidemic

FORMER TORONTO MAYOR JOHN SEWELL—in what was perhaps a slight exaggeration—called 2003 the city's "plague year." In fact, 43 people died of Severe Acute Respiratory Syndrome (SARS) in Toronto, far below the number who die every year of the common flu or air pollution.

That being said, the crisis of SARS shocked Toronto—and the world. There had not been a major disease outbreak in North America since the time of polio in the 1950s, and many feared that SARS would be the next one. The outbreak was to highlight a number of failings in the province's public health system, as patients were misdiagnosed and released from hospital, sometimes with fatal results. There was also particular dismay that all 43 SARS deaths in Canada had occurred in Toronto.

The story of SARS began in China's Guangdong province in November 2002. The identity of the first SARS patient in China—known as Patient #0—remains undisclosed, and the origins of the disease are unknown. Some have speculated that it was an animal disease that mutated into a form that humans could catch, and that the first patient was some sort of farmer or animal handler. Dr. Jiang Yanyong was the first to blow the whistle, when he realized that there were more SARS cases in his hospital than the government claimed existed in the whole country.

The Chinese government was criticized for its early failure to control the disease. The government's secrecy and slow reaction allowed SARS to spread beyond China. The Chinese government later offered an uncharacteristic apology to the world for the slowness of its response and fired a number of its officials, including the health minister and the mayor of Beijing.

Over time, a basic string of symptoms was identified with SARS. Initially, SARS-infected patients seemed to be suffering from the flu. They had coughs, aches, chills and fever, as well as fluid in their lungs. Symptoms usually got worse within a few days, and patients began to have rapid heart rates and memory loss. Hospitalized patients were usually sedated after that point, at which time a tube was inserted into their throat to help them breathe. Some died peacefully, usually after major organ failure, whereas others recovered and later reported having vivid dreams during their period of sedation. Even after making a recovery, they sometimes complained of shortness of breath.

Although only a small number of people became infected by SARS, its mortality rate of 9.6 percent shocked both scientists and the public. For those over 65, the rate went up to 50 percent. No other similar disease kills such a high percentage of its victims.

Antibiotics and antivirals have both proved ineffective at treating SARS.

The first non-Chinese victim of SARS was an American businessman who was on a plane flying from China to Singapore. He began showing extreme pneumonia-like symptoms during the flight, and the plane was diverted to Vietnam. He died soon afterwards in hospital.

The disease was spreading quickly, both within China and in Hanoi and Singapore, as a result of other passengers on the flight becoming affected. From these places the disease spread across Asia. There was a particularly serious outbreak in Hong Kong's Metropole Hotel. A doctor travelling from mainland China had stayed there and had contracted the disease, which then spread through the hotel's sewage system.

A total of 16 guests at the Metropole Hotel were affected, including Kwan Sui Chu, a 78-year-old grandmother from Scarborough who was visiting family in Hong Kong. Chu contracted SARS on February 21, 2003, and returned to Toronto where she became sick and died at home on March 5. Her son, Tse Chi Kwai, caught the disease from her and went to Scarborough Grace Hospital, where he infected other patients and hospital staff. Doctors had misdiagnosed him with tuberculosis. He died on March 13.

Scarborough Grace Hospital is a small 257-bed institution in northwest Scarborough that is dedicated mainly to births and long-term care. It was ill-equipped to handle the outbreak, and a number of other people became infected there. Joseph Pollack, a 76-year-old retired salesman contracted SARS while staying at the hospital. Again misdiagnosing the illness, doctors sent him home, where he died on March 21. His wife Rose caught the disease, but doctors attributed her symptoms to malnutrition as well as stress related to her husband's death. She died April 12 at Mount Sinai Hospital.

James Dougherty, a 77-year-old retired professor also contracted SARS while at Scarborough Grace Hospital. He was similarly misdiagnosed on March 29, but not before infecting his wife, Florence. Florence Dougherty was then sent to York Central Hospital, where she infected another 80-year-old patient.

Eulalio Samson, an 82-year-old retired janitor, was at Scarborough Grace Hospital to receive treatment for his injured knee when he contracted SARS. He died at Centenary Hospital on April 1. Three weeks later, on April 23, Eulalio's wife Gregoria died without being diagnosed. A family friend also contracted SARS while attending her funeral visitation the next day, dying almost immediately. After that, the city's public health department ordered that all SARS victims be cremated or held in the morgue in sealed bags. Once again, Samson's family members contracted the disease. They were sent to the Lapsley Family Clinic, where a doctor and two other patients caught the disease from them, all dying shortly afterwards. One of the relatives died after flying back to her native Philippines, setting off a massive quarantine and another chain of infections in that country.

Several other deaths occurred at Scarborough Grace, including 74-year-old retired transit worker Luigi Romita, who was misdiagnosed and sent to Mount Sinai Hospital. His best friend contracted the disease while visiting him and died shortly afterwards. A number of staff at Scarborough Grace Hospital contracted the disease and were sent to West Park Healthcare Centre to recover. One nurse, Tecla-Lai Yin Lin, died, as did her husband, who had caught the disease from her.

Toronto was soon in the midst of a panic, and the media ran numerous stories about an incurable flu that was killing hundreds in China and that was spreading locally. Chinatown became a ghost town for the first few weeks of the panic. None of the usual crowds of shoppers were on the street—despite there being no evidence that the disease had occurred there. At the corner of Dundas and Spadina, a man sold surgical masks, and most of the people forced to walk through the area—usually moving as fast as they could—had their faces covered. Even after the scare had passed, the sight of elderly Chinese shoppers wearing surgical masks remained a common one for the next couple of years.

Some shops and restaurants closed down altogether, and local politicians urged Torontonians to continue to support Chinese businesses. However, it soon became clear that the disease had spread beyond the Chinese community and was becoming a city-wide phenomenon.

Of those who had succumbed to SARS in Toronto, all but four were over the age of 60, and all were over 40.

Many were in their 80s and 90s. It became evident that SARS was mainly a disease of the elderly.

With all the remaining cases under quarantine, and every hospital in the city under strict orders to screen each person entering or leaving the building, Toronto declared the disease under control. By the end of April, the city began to relax regulations again. However, the most serious blow—which would subject the city to the worst criticism—was still to come.

A second outbreak of SARS began at the much larger North York General Hospital, with the death of 99-year-old Lewis Huppert on May 1, 2003. Huppert had been in the hospital because of a broken pelvis. It is still unknown what the cause of this outbreak was, despite intensive questioning of all the surviving SARS patients from the Scarborough Grace outbreak.

SARS soon spread throughout North York General, killing 90-year-old Berta Weinstain, formerly one of the top criminal lawyers in the Soviet Union. Her daughter Lidia Bychutsky, and son, Mark Weinstain, both contracted the disease from her and died.

Hospital nurse Nelia Laroza contracted the disease but was able to quickly diagnose it in herself and alerted authorities. The result was a massive quarantine of all the students and staff at her son's school. Unfortunately, Laroza died on June 29.

A number of SARS patients from North York General Hospital had been transferred to the St. John's Rehabilitation Centre, where another mini-outbreak began. Istvan Biro, 67, died there on June 16. Retired taxi driver Maurice Buckner, 57, was in the Centre recovering from a lung transplant. He contracted SARS as well and died on May 29. Buckner's wife bitterly complained to the media about the city's public health department and blamed her husband's death on their lax work to control the disease.

Kitty Chan had just come out of a self-imposed quarantine at home on Mother's Day, after having visited relatives in Hong Kong a few weeks earlier. She finally left the house to visit her son, recovering from leg surgery at St. John's Rehabilitation Centre, only to be infected with SARS there. She died on June 7.

The SARS panic had deep ramifications for Toronto. The city's tourism industry was ruined almost overnight as potential visitors from all over cancelled their trips. A 50-percent drop in hotel reservations was recorded, leading to one-third of Toronto's hotel staff being laid off. Four major international conferences scheduled to be held in the city were cancelled, with an estimated loss of $125 million. Approximate total losses to the tourism industry were tagged at $2 billion.

Several countries advised their citizens not to travel to Toronto, and the World Health Organization (WHO) made dire pronouncements on the city's disease preparedness and advised travellers to stay away (leading to incautious criticism of the WHO by Mayor Mel Lastman). The city tried to fight back and improve its image by hosting a major rock concert, nicknamed "SARSstock," headlined by the Rolling Stones. The concert was a success, though it was unclear if it drew many people from outside of Toronto.

Even today, many hotels and attractions claim that their business has never bounced back—though a strong Canadian dollar may have more to do with this than lingering fears of SARS.

With careful control in Toronto, Asia and elsewhere, the spread of the disease eventually stopped. Toronto's final SARS death occurred on August 11, 2003, when 44-year-old baker Mogjan Tehrani died of the disease. Some continued to suffer from SARS after that, but all patients recovered. There remains no cure or treatment for the disease, though research continues.

Legionnaire's Disease Outbreak

October 2005
Toronto

IT IS UNFORTUNATE THAT THE ELDERLY are often viewed as already having one foot in the grave. In many cases, diseases that prey on the old or infirm are not given the same concern as those that affect children or younger people.

In October 2005, a total of 133 seniors caught Legionnaire's disease at Toronto's Seven Oaks Home for the Aged. Twenty-three of them died. Although it caused over half the number of deaths as the SARS scare, the Legionnaire's outbreak received only a fraction of the attention.

Legionnaire's disease is usually caused by the bacteria *Legionella*, which thrives in warm, moist settings. In the worst cases, it causes pneumonia, which can be deadly among the elderly or those with compromised immune systems. Indeed, the disease got its name from an outbreak of pneumonia that occurred at an American Legion convention in 1976.

Common symptoms of the disease include fever, chills, coughing or headaches. Because of this, the disease is often confused with normal pneumonia, but its effects are much more dangerous.

The Seven Oaks Home for the Aged, in the suburb of Scarborough, suffered an outbreak of the disease because of a faulty air conditioning system. It is known that *Legionella* bacteria can be blown as far as 6 kilometres through moisture in the air. In the seniors' home, the disease was not immediately diagnosed. Despite attempts to isolate residents, bacteria travelled through the air conditioning ducts, infecting more of the seniors who lived there. It is believed that an air conditioning tower, located on the outside of the building, provided an ideal moist space for the bacteria to live and multiply.

The Seven Oaks outbreak proved so deadly that scientists suspected that it might be a new, more deadly variant of Legionnaire's disease, not previously seen. Today, it remains the focus of studies.

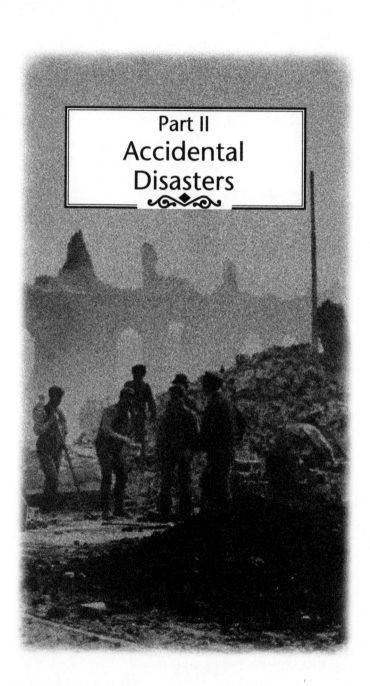

Part II
Accidental
Disasters

York Council Chamber Collapse

IN 1834, YORK WAS ABOUT TO BE INCORPORATED. It was a town of only 9000 people, and its tiny town hall was designed to serve a number of purposes. As well as its main function, the town hall also housed a police station and a small jail.

Facing onto King Street, at the north entrance to the St. Lawrence Market, the town hall was situated in what then was the centre of town. The council chamber sat on the second floor, on top of an enclosed gateway lined with butchers' stalls, which was the entrance to the enclosed market. Above the southern gates on Front Street sat the Market Arms, the town's main inn.

Tragically, Toronto's first town hall was to collapse in the same year that it was built. It served as a government office in York and had been put up in anticipation of the establishment of a city government.

One night, a heated debate was taking place in the council chamber, following a speech by the controversial Radical politician, William Lyon Mackenzie. Mackenzie —a fervent critic of the colonial government of Upper Canada—was preparing to run for mayor of its capital city. Detractors in the crowded council chamber began stamping their feet in unison, shaking the building.

Suddenly, a loud crack was heard, and then a snap. Without further warning, the western end of the council chamber collapsed, dropping the people who had been standing there into the market below.

In all, 24 people were severely injured in the fall, and three were killed. According to legend, they were impaled on meat hooks in the butchers' stalls below. Among the dead was the nephew of Colonel James Fitzgibbon, the hero of the War of 1812. Fitzgibbon was famous for being alerted of the coming American army by Laura Secord.

A week after the disaster, York was formally made a city and renamed "Toronto." Mackenzie, of course, did indeed become elected as its first mayor. The council chamber was repaired, and the building stood until 1849, when it was destroyed by a fire. It was replaced by the majestic St. Lawrence Hall, and a new city hall was built a block south on Front Street, again connected to a rebuilt St. Lawrence Market.

The remains of the second city hall are still visible, incorporated into the modern St. Lawrence Market building. No remains or images of the original city hall are with us today.

Sinking of the *Commerce*

IN THE SMALL HOURS OF MAY 7, 1850, the steamers *Commerce* and *Despatch* collided head-on. The ships were sailing in opposite directions in Lake Erie and hit each other off Port Maitland, at the mouth of the Grand River.

Aboard the *Commerce* were 150 soldiers of the Montréal Welsh Fusiliers, along with their families. The ship was on route to London, Ontario, via Port Stanley, where it was to dock.

It was a calm night, and both ships kept close to the shore, where the waters were shallow. The exact cause of the collision remains a mystery. Both ships were equipped with lights, but this seemed to do little to prevent the catastrophe.

The *Commerce* was totally destroyed in the crash, and it slipped quickly under the 12 metre deep water. The speed of its sinking was surprising, and many aboard had drowned before there was hope of trying to rescue them. The ship suffered a loss of life of between 38 and 41. The army recorded that one officer and 24 soldiers from the Fulisiers, as well as 13 of their wives and children had drowned. The others lost in the accident were presumably crew members.

Most of the passengers survived, however, thanks to the work of the *Minos*, a government-owned steamer that had raced out to rescue whoever it could. The *Minos'* crew also later helped with the recovery of bodies.

The *Despatch*, damaged, still managed to crawl back to port.

When the rescue effort was completed, fingers were quickly pointed at the captains of the vessels. In fact, the accusations were serious enough that local magistrates put them under arrest. They were recorded as being charged with the "killing of the 41 individuals that perished with the *Commerce*." The court released them both on bail, with the order to return to the Niagara Court of Assizes to stand trial.

A grand jury was assembled to try the two men. In the end, Captain Cochrane of the *Commerce* was acquitted of all charges and released. When the second trial was to begin, however, Captain McSwain of the *Despatch* was nowhere to be found. Despite putting up $500 for his bail, he appeared to have fled the country. Where he had gone was never discovered. When it became clear that McSwain would not return, the grand jury was released and his trial remained unfinished.

As for the *Despatch* itself, the ship was repaired and put back to work. However, it sank in 1859 while sailing in the Thames River. It was salvaged and repaired once again. Its new name was *Reindeer*.

Sinking of the *Atlantic*

August 20, 1852
Lake Erie

ONE OF THE MOST BIZARRE SHIPPING DISASTERS in the Great Lakes—a kind of maritime hit-and-run—occurred in 1852. The propeller boat *Ogdensburgh* collided with the huge steamboat *Atlantic*, just off Long Point, on Lake Erie's northern shore. The *Atlantic* was the fastest passenger ship on the Great Lakes at the time and was overloaded with passengers, mainly European immigrants seeking a new life in North America.

Sometime between 2:30 and 3 AM, *Ogdensburgh* crashed its bow into the hull of the *Atlantic*. Erik Thorstad, a Norwegian immigrant, later reported, "When it was about half past two o'clock in the morning I awoke with a heavy shock. Immediately suspecting that another boat had run into ours, I hastened up at once. Since there was great confusion and fright among the passengers I asked several if our boat had been damaged. But I did not get any reassuring answer."

Thorstad watched a lifeboat being filled with passengers from the lower decks. As it was set into the lake, it took on water and sank, killing all those who had climbed in. Immediately after that, water began rushing into the *Atlantic* itself, and, in Thorstad's words, "a pitiful cry arose" from the doomed passengers.

The *Ogdensburgh* had neglected to stop at the scene of the accident or to enquire as to the state of the *Atlantic* with its captain. Had this happened, it is likely that everyone on board could have been rescued before the *Atlantic* went down. Instead, the *Ogdensburgh* simply continued on its course across Lake Erie to Buffalo, New York.

Captain Pettey of the *Atlantic* was knocked down several decks into a lifeboat and suffered a concussion. He was too badly injured to coordinate the rest of the rescue, and nobody else stepped in to take control.

The *Atlantic* was soon at a 45-degree angle, resting on a large pocket of air. As this air was forced out, the ship sank deeper into the water. Luckily, the fleeing *Ogdensburgh*—by this time 3 kilometres away—heard the screams of the *Atlantic* passengers and decided to turn back. It was able to rescue the majority of the passengers. However, between 150 and 250 had already drowned (the ship's passenger list was also lost, so no clear figure was ever put on the dead).

Almost as dramatic as the sinking of the *Atlantic* are the many attempts that have been made to salvage parts of it. Later in 1852, an experimental submarine—the first in Lake Erie—attempted to explore the wreck. However, it too sank. Other salvage attempts were made in 1854, 1855, 1873 and 1910. In 1856, the ship's safe was brought to the surface. In 1989, a private consortium of explorers rediscovered the wreck and tried to claim it for themselves, believing that valuable cargo might still be buried in it. They were successfully sued by the Canadian government, which traditionally controls the ownership of sunken vessels. Since 1996, the government has held undisputed ownership of the *Atlantic* but has shown no interest in excavating it.

Sinking of the *Ocean Wave*

❧◆❧

April 30, 1853
Lake Ontario

ON ROUTE FROM OGDENSBURG, NEW YORK, to Toronto, the *Ocean Wave* caught fire at 2 AM on April 30. The ship sunk 5 kilometres from False Duck Island's Traverse Point on Lake Ontario, not far from Kingston.

It was later guessed that—because the *Ocean Wave* was a steamer powered by an old wood-burning engine— some sparks had shot out of the smoke stack. The ship carried a load of hams, ash, butter, flour, seeds and tallow. The tallow in particular was highly flammable, and likely sped up the movement of the fire across the ship.

Its upper portion was reduced to ashes within 10 to 15 minutes. Within another 15 minutes, the hull was also destroyed. The speed of the flames prevented the normal emergency procedures from being followed. Initially, the ship's captain had tried to steer it for shore, but the gears stopped working, causing it to drift without power some 13 kilometres from the shore. The fire forced the pilot away from the wheel and burned the lifeboats before they could be lowered.

Given all this, it is remarkable that anyone survived the sinking of the *Ocean Wave*. Two nearby ships—the *Emblem* and the *Georgina*—were quick to arrive on the scene and picked up passengers floating on debris in the lake. Between 23 and 36 people died from burns or drowning.

After the sinking had happened, the wreck became the focus of interest. It was revealed that as well as its usual load of food items, the *Ocean Wave* was also carrying the previous year's earnings for the company that owned it. Because currency was often unreliable in those days, the earnings had been converted into silver and gold bars. In 1857, divers managed to salvage the previous metals, and the exact location of the wreck was quickly forgotten. It was rediscovered by divers in 1991.

Baptiste Creek Train Collision

October 27, 1854
Kent County

SOME DAYS, IT SEEMS AS THOUGH EVERYTHING goes disastrously wrong. October 27, 1854, seems to have been one of those days.

The Great Western Railway company had noticed that a portion of their new track, near Chatham, had been weakened due to erosion. The route had been inaugurated just earlier that year, providing the first link between Windsor, London, Hamilton and Niagara Falls. A gravel train was ordered to the area from London, so that workers could shore up the ballast under the track.

On the same day that the gravel train left, a Great Western express passenger train—which was "express" in name only, considering that it was running a horrendous seven hours behind schedule—was headed from London to Windsor.

At 1 PM, due to a signalling error, the two trains collided at Baptiste Creek, 21 kilometres west of Windsor, in rural Kent County. The force of the collision was incredible. The passenger train was travelling at a speed of 32 kilometres per hour, considered to be rather fast at the time. The gravel train was moving more slowly, and with 15 cars of gravel, it was a virtually immovable object.

In heavy fog, the passenger train hit the back of the gravel train. The locomotive and express cars of the gravel train were thrown completely off the track and smashed into pieces. The first- and second-class cars in the passenger train were splintered, while the third-class car was flattened. Ultimately, however, it was the second-class car that received the most damage, with most of its occupants crushed by the collapsing walls and ceiling. The survivors came away with horrific injuries, such as amputated limbs. Passengers in the final cars, behind third-class, survived, mostly of them unhurt.

On the gravel train, the conductor who had been positioned at the back of the last car to hold up the light barely survived. When he realized that the engineer on the passenger train had not seen his lamp in time, he leapt to safety, just seconds before the crash. Unfortunately, the young boy who worked as his assistant was not so fast, and he was crushed to death by the speeding locomotive.

The wreck was such a mess of twisted metal and wood, mixed up with humans and body parts, that it took rescuers four hours to remove all the passengers from it. Many of the bodies were horribly mangled together.

In the end, 52 people were killed and 58 injured, making it the worst railway accident in North American history at that time.

"There was one woman buried under a mass of ruins, and lay there over four hours before she was extricated," *The Globe* quoted a witness as saying.

> *We were 32 miles from Detroit and 13 from Chatham, the surrounding country for miles a vast swamp, and no aid and physicians at hand, which with the denseness of the fog and frightful screams of the wounded for help and water, rendered it the most appalling scene imaginable. It was heart sickening. Yet all was done that could be, during the five hours that the miserable unfortunates lay waiting their turn for assistance. One man had six friends with him, all killed.*

Although fog was considered the main culprit of the collision, the gravel train was largely held to blame.

Its engineer had kept the train moving too slowly, expecting the passenger train to pass on an alternate track. A watchman who had been sent out by the gravel train to look for oncoming trains in the fog apparently fell asleep on the job.

Today, fog continues to harass travellers in exactly the same part of Kent county. Although train schedules and upgraded signalling systems are now computerized, and collisions rarely happen, the spot is infamous for automobile pileups on the 401 highway.

Sinking of the *Northern Indiana*

July 17, 1856
Lake Erie

THE AMERICAN SHIP *NORTHERN INDIANA* was on route from Buffalo to Toledo, passing through Canadian waters on July 17, 1856. The modern sidewheel steamer, built only four years earlier, was carrying 175 passengers. It caught fire 10 kilometres off Point Pelee, and most of the ship burned. At first, passengers and crew piled into the ship's lifeboats. However, because the paddlewheels of the *Northern Indiana* were still turning, all the lifeboats had flipped over. Many of the people in the lifeboats were sucked into the paddlewheels and crushed. A number of other passengers on the *Northern Indiana* jumped overboard and were rescued by the *Mississippi* and *Republic*, which happened to be nearby.

Once the fire was extinguished, the *Republic* tried to tow the *Northern Indiana* to shore at Point Pelee, but to no avail. The ship was too badly damaged and sunk on the way, just before reaching the shore, its top still sticking out of the shallow waters. Its engines and boilers were hauled up in September 1856 for salvage.

Between 30 and 60 people died. The exact number remains unknown, because the *Northern Indiana*'s passenger list was burned during the fire. Bodies continued to wash up on the shore of Essex and Kent counties for weeks afterwards.

The exact cause of the fire that sunk the ship was never discovered.

The *Buffalo Republic* printed a detailed description of the sinking of the *Northern Indiana*. According to the newspaper, *Northern Indiana* and *Mississippi* left Buffalo together. When they got to Point Pelee, *Northern Indiana* pulled ahead. Captain Langley of the *Mississippi* was on deck with friends, enjoying the good weather, when he noticed smoke coming out of the starboard gangway of the *Northern Indiana*. Langley ordered the *Mississippi*'s engineer to speed her up and bring her alongside the *Northern Indiana*. Langley lowered his ship's lifeboats so that they could be used to pick up passengers from the *Northern Indiana* and bring them to safety.

By this time, however, the *Northern Indiana* had stopped moving and was engulfed in flames. Its passengers were crowded on deck, screaming and crying to be saved. Others had jumped in the water, some clinging to bits of debris. Events happened so suddenly that things quickly became chaotic. One crew member from the *Mississippi*, John McDonough, jumped into the water and pulled several drowning people to safety. Many others, unfortunately, could not be saved in time. As with many disasters involving 19th-century passenger ships, most of the victims were female, pulled down by the weight of their elaborate dresses.

Desjardins Canal Bridge Collapse

◆

March 17, 1857
Desjardins Canal, Wentworth County

THE DESJARDINS CANAL WAS COMPLETED IN 1837, connecting the town of Dundas, near Hamilton, with Burlington Bay. When the first railway was constructed in Ontario, a bridge was built over the canal.

By 1857, the bridge was publicly known to be in poor repair, and discussions about repairing or replacing it had begun. What the public did not know was that the wooden bridge was actually rotten and in much worse shape than anyone had imagined. The result was one of the worst and most dramatic railway disasters of Canadian history.

On March 17, 1857—St. Patrick's Day—a Great Western passenger train passed over the bridge. For reasons that remain unknown, the train's engine derailed while on the bridge, possibly because of a broken axle. The shift in weight was too much for the weakened timbers of the bridge to support. The entire structure collapsed into the still frozen canal almost 20 metres below, taking the train with it.

The engine and tender broke through 61 centimetres of ice to reach the water below, while the baggage car flipped and landed on the shore of the canal. The first passenger car somersaulted in the air and landed upside down on the ice, breaking through. The second car landed on its end.

No one in the swampy rural area directly witnessed the collapse. A railway worker farther down the line reported seeing smoke puffs coming from the engine as it

In one of Canada's most dramatic rail disasters, the bridge over the Desjardins Canal collapsed in 1857, sending a train and its passengers through the ice below.

crossed the bridge. Suddenly the smoke stopped. When he went to investigate, he quickly discovered what had happened and alerted the authorities.

Rescuers from Hamilton rushed to the area and worked throughout the rest of the day and night, in harsh weather, to aid survivors and recover bodies. Amazingly, some 30 people survived the dramatic crash. They included a number of passengers from the second car and four of the five railway staff who had been riding in the baggage car. All the passengers in the first car were killed, as were the engineer and fireman, whose bodies were found much later at the bottom of the canal. The men had been thrown out of the engine and then crushed by it.

Approximately 60 people died in the accident, including the railway and real estate magnate Samuel Zimmerman, thought to have been the richest man in Canada at the time.

Although plans were drawn up to rebuild the bridge after the disaster, the public was unconvinced about the safety of a new bridge, and protest against the idea killed it. The Desjardins Canal proved to be an economic failure for shipping and was abandoned soon afterwards. The canal filled with sediment and eventually ceased to exist. The new railway line between Toronto and Hamilton was constructed in a different route. Today, the overgrown and still-rotting remains of the bridge over the Desjardins Canal can be seen. The area around the bridge has become a park, part of Cootes Paradise and the Royal Botanical Gardens.

Sinking of the *Bavarian*

<hr>

November 5, 1873
Lake Ontario

THE STEAMBOAT *KINGSTON* WAS originally built in 1855. After a fire gutted it in 1872, it was reconstructed and given a new name, the *Bavarian*. As both *Kingston* and *Bavarian*, the boat plied the waters of eastern Lake Ontario and the Thousand Islands. It was a passenger ship, bringing both the wealthy and the poor on practical journeys and sightseeing tours.

On November 5, 1873, the ship was on a journey east from Toronto, heading for the St. Lawrence. While the *Bavarian* was passing Bowmanville, a fire broke out on board. As the *Toronto Mail* reported, "All of a sudden the cry of 'Fire!' was heard, and instantaneously, as though the lightning had struck her, the *Bavarian* was wreathed in flames…. The number of persons were so limited, the night so comparatively fine, with the moon shining in a clear frosty sky, and the water little more than ruffled by the breeze, that the tragic end which has befallen fourteen persons, including three lady passengers, appears incredible."

It seemed that a beam had broken loose in the hold of the ship and smashed down onto the 25 barrels of liquor that the *Bavarian* was transporting. The beam broke the barrels open and sent their contents down onto the coal-burning furnace below, where the liquid caught fire. Witnesses noticed the ship burning with an eerie blue flame, the colour of an alcohol-fed fire.

The ship's pilot and eight of the crew quickly lowered one lifeboat and jumped into it. Other crew members tried to lower another boat, but it slipped off its ropes into the water and became swamped. A third lifeboat was virtually thrown into the water, landing upright. The first mate and a dozen others jumped into this boat. The plug was missing from the bottom of the rowboat though, and it nearly sunk before someone could find it!

The ship's captain was seen floating on a plank with a life preserver. He paddled over to the first mate's boat but was told to wait a minute before coming on board—they had to plug the leak first. A boy who had been floating on the same plank as the captain hopped in the lifeboat anyway. The captain then pushed off, presumably heading for the pilot's boat, where there was no room. The captain was never seen again.

Fourteen of the *Bavarian*'s 36 passengers perished, but the ship's story was not over yet.

Although most of the ship was destroyed, its hull was salvaged yet again. After being rebuilt in Kingston, it was renamed *Algerian* and launched once more. In 1904, it was renovated and renamed *Cornwall*. Finally, in 1930, the ship was dismantled, and its hull scuttled off Amhert Island in the St. Lawrence River.

Victoria Capsize

May 24, 1881
Thames River, near London, Ontario

IT WAS A PLEASANT EARLY SUMMER AFTERNOON and most Londoners were celebrating the Victoria Day weekend. The holiday had more significance then—after all, Queen Victoria was still alive (it was her 62nd birthday). Many people had decided to go to Springbank Park, a 30-minute boat ride down the Thames River from the main Sulphur Springs docks. The park (now the largest in London and known as Chestnut Park) was a popular picnic spot, built around the city's waterworks.

Three steamboats plied the muddy water of the Thames, ferrying passengers between the city and the park. One of them, *Forest City*, ran aground on a sandbar, and its passengers had to be picked up by the *Queen Victoria*.

When the *Queen Victoria* (known as *Victoria* for short) returned to Sulphur Springs, the next round of passengers was upset about the delay. The crowd rushed the boat, knocking over the ticket collector. Not wanting to make the situation worse by delaying any longer, and glad to collect the fares they could, the crew of the *Victoria* set sail with the rowdy passengers on board. In total, the small ferry now had some 600 people on board—three times its intended capacity. Many of the passengers headed for the upper decks, making the steamboat dangerously top heavy.

The *Victoria*'s captain noticed that the boat was sailing lower in the water than usual. Crowds of children began running from one side of the boat to the other, causing it to tip back and forth. The boat sunk lower and lower in the water.

At some point, it is believed that the bottom of the boat scraped on rocks underwater, though no one specifically noticed the incident. Water began leaking in through the bottom of the *Victoria*. Because the boat was so crowded, the crew was unable to communicate the danger to everybody in time. Most didn't realize that the boat was sinking until the first deck went underwater. Even after that, some of the people on the upper deck were unaware of what was happening. However, as the realization started to spread across the crowd, they quickly began to panic.

The frantic movement of passengers caused the boat to tip further, and the steam boiler came crashing down, badly burning many of the crowd and weakening the supports for the upper deck. Soon the upper deck collapsed on top of the lower deck, and a fight broke out among the passengers as they kicked and punched each other to be the first to get away from the boat.

An estimated 182 passengers drowned—125 of them children—only metres from shore. The actual number of dead was never confirmed. Many bodies were washed downstream, never to be found, and several women, burdened by the heavy Victorian dresses that were fashionable at the time, simply sunk and were not seen again.

One passenger, Samuel Glass, saved many others by dragging them to the riverbank. The water was so shallow that he could actually stand on the bottom of the river and keep his head out of the water.

Some of those who made it to the shore faced an unfriendly welcome. A farmer, whose property edged the river, not only refused to help the survivors but also unsympathetically ordered them to stop trespassing on his land. He was only convinced of the error of his position when some of the survivors, led by the intimidating butcher John Mitcheltree, made a noose, strung it up from a tree and prepared to hang him.

The nearby steamboat *Princess Louise* picked up other survivors, but it eventually also did the job of recovering bodies, a task that lasted through the night and into the next day.

Almost as disastrous as the sinking of the *Victoria* itself was the savagery of the recovery effort. Some of the volunteers who had showed up to assist in the rescue effort had less than friendly intentions—such as stealing the wallets and purses of the deceased. Likewise, of the army of carts and wagons that delivered the dead bodies to the homes of their relatives, some drivers charged outrageous fees for their services. Other drivers—on finding no one home—simply threw the corpses through the door and then left to find more. One corpse was apparently left sitting on a chair on a relative's porch with a note pinned to it.

Queen Victoria herself sent condolences over the disaster, and many Londoners wore black armbands for the following month in memory of the dead. A committee was quickly formed to raise a relief fund. It included the famous London brewers John Labatt and John Carling.

The passengers who survived the *Victoria* sinking blamed the captain and shipowners for the disaster, while the owners blamed reckless passengers. The government inquiry into the sinking later declared that no one in particular was to blame for it. The disaster had been caused by "hurry and money-making, the twin curses of an age of over-excitement."

The sudden decline in popularity of the river ferries left Springbank Park virtually empty on future Victoria Days. That is, until 1896 when a new streetcar line was laid down, connecting London and the park. Soon, people returned to have picnics there once again.

High Park Train Wreck

January 2, 1884
Toronto

THE COMPLEX NATURE OF TRAIN SCHEDULES may be hard enough for experienced engineers to understand, but it can have deadly consequences for inexperienced ones. Such a tragedy occurred on January 2, 1884, in the west end of Toronto.

Junior engineer Richard Jeffry was called to work on New Year's Day and told to lead an empty freight train into Toronto. This job made him uncomfortable—no doubt because he had only recently begun the job and had never driven into Toronto, with its complex network of lines, junctions and signals.

Jeffry requested a "pilot"—an experienced crewman—to help him with the job. For unknown reasons, the Great Western Railway turned down the request.

After starting the trip in southwestern Ontario, Jeffry reached Hamilton by the morning of January 2. There he received vague instructions for the rest of the journey. "Run to Queen's Wharf, avoiding regulars" was the message from the railway company management. Already tired—having worked 18 hours straight—Jeffry pushed ahead.

He expected to meet only one other train, a mail and express, near Oakville. In fact, a more careful reading of the schedule for that day would have showed that a commuter train was heading towards Jeffry's train, from Queen's Wharf station—on the same track.

In freezing cold temperatures and blizzard conditions, Jeffry and his freight train left Hamilton for Toronto at 5:20 AM. The commuter train left Queen's Wharf for Mimico at 6:49 AM.

Jeffry passed Mimico station. Normally, the station staff would have flagged him down and forced him to switch to another track, but the station was unmanned until 7:30 AM.

"As soon as I heard her whistle I knew there was going to be an accident, and I ran down the road," said John Donovan of the Toronto Bolt and Iron Works. It was beside that factory, close to Toronto's High Park, that the trains collided head-on at 6:57 AM. Both were steaming ahead at 80 kilometres per hour. The blizzard conditions prevented them from seeing each other until they were only 280 metres apart—nowhere near the distance required to stop.

Engineer John Kennedy of the commuter train pulled the brakes and ordered the steam cut to prevent an explosion. Then he and his brakeman, James Gasken, jumped off the engine and ran as far away as they could.

The *Toronto Mail* reported:

> The heavy freight locomotive, backed by a tender fully laden with coal and water, together with the caboose and baggage car, dashed up against the comparatively light dummy. The boiler of the latter was carried completely off its wheels and, followed by the freight locomotive, smashed into the first passenger coach. So great was the velocity and consequent momentum of the ponderous freight engine that it mounted the trucks of the smaller engine, and running clean over them followed the boiler into the car. Strange to say the sides of the latter were almost intact. It was one of the most complete telescope accidents ever known. The wheels did not even leave the track and the rails were in no wise injured.

The paper added that the roofs of the passenger cars were utterly pulverized, leaving no piece of wood bigger than 15 centimetres. One passenger, John Carrigan, who was sitting at the front of the car, was actually thrown through the roof. Although his body was full of splinters, he survived.

Many more did not survive the awful crash. In all, 29 were killed—15 on the scene, 10 later that day in hospital and 4 in the following days. The only crew member of the freight train to die was Charles Thomas, the fireman. The other dead were employees of Toronto Bolt and Iron Works. The youngest killed were teenage workers—as young as 13—commuting to the westend factory. Two sets of brothers also died.

People from the factory quickly rushed out to help their co-workers. However, a fire that had broken out in the wreck had to be put out before rescuers could get close to the scene. Another commuter train heading for the area was stopped and loaded with wounded passengers, so they could be taken back downtown to the hospital.

A coroner's inquest was held on January 15. It blamed Jeffry's inexperience, the railway company's refusal to assign him a pilot and the lack of staff at Mimico station. Jeffry was charged with manslaughter, as was the freight train's brakeman. However, they were judged not guilty, because the crash had been an accident that had threatened both of their lives as well.

In those days, disability pay did not exist, and only the wealthiest could afford insurance. Therefore, many injured factory workers found themselves without a livelihood because of the crash. However, coverage in the local newspapers brought attention to their plight, and several fundraising events were held to assist the workers.

John Holderness, owner of the Black Horse Hotel, donated nearly 2000 kilograms of beef to the victims, with the assistance of the St. Lawrence Market's butchers. The governor general donated $250. The famed Toronto engineer Colonel Casimir Gzowski (great-great grandfather of broadcaster Peter Gzowski) donated $100, while the Toronto Bolt and Iron Works donated another $100. In all, $8072.73 was raised—a huge sum at the time.

St. Thomas Train Wreck

PORT STANLEY, WITH ITS BEACHES AND PARKS, has long been a favourite vacation spot for Londoners. However, on July 15, 1887, disaster struck a group of Londoners as they were returning home from a day of relaxation.

At 6:40 PM, a northbound Grand Trunk Railway train from Port Stanley was passing through St. Thomas. Its 10 cars were overwhelmed with passengers—over 400 in all—and it was standing-room only.

At a speed of 60 kilometres per hour, the express train approached St. Thomas' junction. A new railway signal had been installed there, but it was not yet working. With its power turned off, it remained in the default mode: all clear. The train's engineer, Henry Donnelly—a veteran with nearly 50 years' experience—apparently failed to realize the danger and kept the engine going.

The Michigan Central Railway owned the intersecting railway line. At the same moment that the passenger train was heading towards the railway intersection, a freight train pulling boxcars and petroleum tank cars was heading west along that route.

By the time Donnelly was close enough the see the freight train, it was too late. He pulled on the air brakes, but nothing happened—they appeared to be broken. He then ordered his brakemen to operate the handbrakes, and he threw the engine into reverse. However, even though the wheels were no longer turning forward, momentum kept the train squealing ahead. Two of the train's crew leapt off the engine to save themselves.

At approximately 7 PM, the Grand Trunk engine slammed into the side of one of the freight train's petroleum cars. It immediately exploded in a fireball that engulfed the engine, baggage car and front passenger cars.

Panic ensued as the surviving passengers rushed to escape the train, crawling through windows and crowded doorways. Fire crews were on the scene almost immediately, apparently unaware of the danger that they faced. Unable to build up enough pressure in their hoses, they could do little to fight the intensity of the fire—or prevent it from spreading to the other petroleum cars.

Only 10 minutes later, a second petroleum car exploded, sending flames 100 metres in the air and almost instantly burning alive one of the firefighters. Nearby buildings also caught fire, and the blaze began to spread into St. Thomas. The force of the blast shattered windows as far as four blocks away. Panicked horses in the town began to run wild, trampling and killing a woman. It was not until two hours later that the fire was brought under control.

In all, 17 people were killed in the explosions and fire, including Donnelly. Many of the other victims were young children, returning with their families from a day at the beach.

By the next day, souvenir seekers were combing through the wreckage. The *London Advertiser* noted, "Every other or third man met in St. Thomas seems to wear some mark of the explosion in the way of plasters, bandages, slings, etc. ... Scores of hats were picked up near the scene of the wreck and explosion, where they had been lost by the owners in their mad flight to escape.

The road bed for a block around is also littered with remnants of burned clothing torn from the backs of the injured spectators."

An inquest into the crash was held between July 18 and August 2. Initial suspicions that Donnelly had been drunk were rejected by witnesses. Most agreed that he could not be blamed, though the train might have been moving too quickly in a populated district.

It was also suggested that there might have been a kink in the air brakes, preventing them from working. The conductor, whose job it had been to inspect the brakes before leaving Port Stanley, was charged with manslaughter, but the charge was later dropped. The families of many of the victims were outraged at the Grand Trunk Railway and demanded that charges be made against its directors. In the end, however, little came out of the inquest.

The picturesque town of Port Stanley is still a favourite of Londoners and others, and is served by a short railway line that caters to tourists and cottagers.

London City Hall Collapse

January 3, 1898
London

THE CITY HALL IN LONDON, ONTARIO, was built in 1854, the same year the city was incorporated. At the time, Ontario, like most parts of North America, had no building codes. This resulted in a number of preventable tragedies—some of them recorded in this book—including fires, disease outbreaks due to poor sanitation, and deadly collapses.

By the end of the 19th century, London had grown tremendously. It was easily the largest city in western Ontario. Over time, demands for more space were put on the city hall as more city staff were hired. An addition to the building had been built in the 1880s. In 1893, the province's first building code came into effect, but it was ignored when, in the mid 1890s, the mayor's office was renovated. Fatefully, the wall that supported the second floor auditorium was removed during the renovations and replaced with a wooden beam 30 centimetres thick.

On the cold night of January 3, 1898, the result of this poor (and illegal) decision was felt in the most dramatic way. A municipal election had taken place that day in London. By 9:30 PM, the city hall was packed with the supporters of Mayor Dr. John Wilson, to hear his victory speeches. As many as 2500 people squeezed into the standing-room-only auditorium, pushing it beyond capacity. Alderman R.M.C. Toothe was approaching the podium to make a speech when a loud crack was heard across the room. It was the sound of the 30-centimetre beam snapping.

After a few seconds of shocked silence, the northeast corner of the floor collapsed. Spectators were sent crashing down to the floor below—ending up, of all places, in the city engineer's office. Soon, other parts of the floor began to cave in, sending 250 people down with it, as well as a 225-kilogram safe and a massive—and burning hot—cast iron radiator.

"Now this is going to be a horrible death!" exclaimed Toothe, as he fell, head-first, into the newly formed hole. The people who had gathered on the temporary platform around the podium fell backwards through the floor, causing the platform to rock forwards and crumple. The room quickly filled with plaster dust, making it impossible to see.

"I instantly abandoned all hope of being alive more than two or three minutes...for a time all was black before my eyes," wrote reporter Harry Atkinson. He himself had fallen through the floor. "I saw the face of the little boy who had sat near me at the table. He was lying beside me and crying for his mother.... Other faces were very close to me, but I recognized none. They were partly covered with blood and, more frightful still, with expressions of agony."

"I could hardly sleep that night and the horror remains with me still," wrote former MP Robert Boston. In the wild panic to escape the building, he was one of the first out. Along with his brother, a retired firefighter, he led the initial rescue efforts.

Although some details of the collapse may seem comical, it was a disaster of serious proportions. No less than 23 people were killed in the fall and crush of other crowd members and debris. Another 150 were seriously wounded. Rescuers found bodies and wounded victims mixed together, layered seven or eight deep. It took more than two hours to extract everyone from the horrible scene.

Mayor Wilson also fell through the floor, but he managed to escape with only bruises.

John Burridge, who had survived London's other great disaster—the sinking of the ferry *Queen Victoria*—had been on the ground floor at the time of the collapse. He was killed by the falling safe, his skull so badly crushed that he could only be identified by the cut of his beard.

London's chief city engineer—who had overseen the renovations—stubbornly refused to accept blame. He told *The Globe* that it was the crowd who were at fault.

> *I am of opinion that the pressure of the mass of humanity into the northeast corner on and around the (speaker's) platform and on the seats, and the tremendous stamping of feet on the floor by the very excited crowd, supplied the pressure and the jar to cause an abnormal demand on the strength of the supports.... It was the tremendous dead weight around the platform that caused the collapse.*

Even after this terrible event, London stubbornly continued to ignore the new building codes. It was not until another collapse 10 years later—in which a theatre, Reid's Crystal Hall, caved in—that the bylaws were finally put into practice.

Ottawa-Hull Fire

THE NATIONAL CAPITAL'S MOST SERIOUS FIRE occurred in 1900, beginning across the river in Québec. On the morning of April 26, the home of Antoine Kirouac caught on fire near downtown Hull (today officially known as Gatineau). It was later suspected that a spark from Kirouac's chimney set one of the wooden shingles on his roof on fire. Soon, the entire neighbourhood, largely made up of similar small, wooden houses, was ablaze as winds fanned the fire.

By noon, most of downtown Hull was destroyed, and the fire was spreading to lumber yards near the Ottawa River. Thirteen hundred homes had been destroyed, and 40 percent of the population would be homeless by the end of the night. Fire crews simply gave up and fled the city, and even the fire station burned.

Many of the desperate gathered inside the stone walls of Hull's Catholic church, praying for the wind to die down. At the end of the day, the church was the only public building in the town to survive the fire.

Crowds gathered on Parliament Hill to watch the fire in Hull, convinced that the Ontario side of the river would be safe. However, sparks from the burning wood were blown all the way across to lumber yards in Ottawa. By 2 PM, most of Ottawa's warehouses and mills, located along the river and in the Lebreton Flats area, were on fire. The CPR station was burned, as was the grain elevator of McKay Milling and the powerhouses that supplied electricity to Ottawa and its local electric railway system. The entire industrial district of Ottawa, Chaudière, was wiped out, along with the nearby neighbourhoods of Mechanicsville and Hintonburg

Rochesterville—one of Ottawa's most elite neighbour-hoods—was the next to catch fire. Logging baron J.R. Booth lost both his massive home and his lumberyard, located near the river. The fire then began to move inland to the Ministry of Agriculture's Experimental Farm. Fire-fighters, including crews from Montréal and Kingston, were busy hosing down buildings that had not yet caught fire, in the hopes of protecting them.

The flames came close to engulfing Parliament, and the trees covering the edge of Parliament Hill, going down to the river, were mostly burned. Diligent firefighters managed to save the buildings (though fire would get its revenge 10 years later, when the Parliament Fire would destroy the Centre Block).

In the end, downtown Ottawa was saved by pure luck. The *Evening Journal* reported that "If the wind had not changed direction, all the firemen and all the engines in Canada would never have stayed the progress eastward." Firefighters continued to struggle against the blaze past dark; it was eventually put out around midnight.

On the evening of the fire, Franklin Gadsby, a journalist for the *Canadian Magazine*, was watching the scene. "I note one roof after another twinkle, glow and burst into garish effulgence. The millions of feet of lumber all along the riverbanks are alight. The lurid, enfouldred smoke floats in dense plumes over Parliament Hill and towers of the national buildings," he wrote.

Even as the tail end of the fire raged, drunken looting was happening in the city. Taverns had apparently stayed open until the last moment, and the army had to be deployed to restore order.

In Ottawa, over 300 hectares of the city had been destroyed, 2000 homes had been burned to the ground and 8000 people were homeless. Over 30 million metres of logs had been turned into charcoal, and total damages to the city were estimated in the millions of dollars.

It was considered lucky that only seven people had died on the Ottawa side of the river.

The Interprovincial Bridge between Ottawa and Hull, in the middle of construction at the time, was at first thought to have been destroyed by the fire. On later inspection, it was found to be badly damaged, with its steel warped from the heat, but still capable of being repaired. In December 1900, the first train crossed the Interprovincial Bridge, at that time the longest cantilever bridge in the world. It is still in use today.

Donations began to pour in after the fire to support those who had lost their homes and jobs, and to help rebuild the city. The General Relief Committee that was set up by the City of Ottawa collected nearly $1 million in donations. The federal government made $100,000 in funding available, and Lord Mayor of London organized the donation of $200,000 to rebuild Ottawa (including money directly given by Queen Victoria). Smaller amounts came from other places across the country and abroad. The City of St. John's, Newfoundland, donated $402.07, and Victoria, BC, gave $110. At the bottom of the list of donations recorded was one from a Mrs. Florence J. Walters of Valparaiso, Chile, who was marked down as sending $4.86.

A trainload of in-kind donations came from the T. Eaton Company in Toronto, and a Chicago meat-packing company contributed thousands of kilograms of pork and beef.

The village of Portland, Ontario (population 37), gave 183 bushels of potatoes to the people of Ottawa. And for those who hadn't seen enough smoke to last them a lifetime, the Empire Tobacco Company donated 1000 kilograms of tobacco.

By the end of 1900, 445 new homes had been built in Ottawa and 29 were on their way to being finished. The CPR had also rebuilt its shops and station by the Ottawa River. Rochesterville, however, would never see its past glory restored, and most of Ottawa's wealthy citizens who had lived there chose to move to the Rockliffe Park area on the other side of the city.

Wanstead Train Crash

December 26, 1902
Wanstead (Lambton County)

SOME ACCIDENTS SEEM ALMOST FATED TO HAPPEN, capable of foiling any number of attempts to prevent them.

In 1902, Wanstead was a small village on a major railway line—as it still is today. The lines connected Toronto with the industrial city of Sarnia, before crossing the St. Clair River to Port Huron, Michigan.

On Boxing Day of that year, railway company dispatchers were struggling to deal with the increased number of trains as well as passengers returning home from spending Christmas with relatives. Two trains heading in opposite directions, one freight and one passenger, needed to pass along a single line at the same time. It was decided that they would meet at the town of Wyoming, not far from Wanstead. There, one of them would temporarily switch onto a siding to allow the other to safely pass.

However, a snowstorm had kept the passenger train running late. Dispatcher James G. Kerr was keen not to delay it any further—after all, one of its passengers was his boss, District Supervisor W.E. Costello. From his office in London, Kerr telegraphed local stations at 9:48 PM to inform them that the trains would pass farther east, at Wanstead rather than Wyoming.

Minutes later, though, at 9:57, it appeared that the freight train might also be running late. Kerr telegraphed the passenger train to tell it that the plans to pass at Wanstead might be cancelled. Due to some miscommunication, the train's engineer understood that the orders were definitely cancelled and that he should push on to Wyoming.

Kerr wired the freight train and told it to proceed to Wanstead, not understanding how the orders to the passenger train had been interpreted. Shortly thereafter, he realized the danger of what was about to happen and tried to wire both trains to stop—but they had already left the stations and were beyond communication.

Desperate, Kerr contacted the tiny station of Kingsford Junction, between Wanstead and the speeding freight train. The only railway employee at Kingsford Junction was 17-year-old James Troyer, working his third day on the job. The teen had trouble understanding the signal, and it took him between seven and eight minutes to pass on the message to the freight train. By this point, the passenger train was travelling at 80 kilometres per hour.

With difficulty, however, the freight was able to slow down and prepared to move onto the siding. But a frozen switch, which had to be manually warmed up while the train waited on the main track, delayed the move.

At 10:10 PM, just as the freight train was finally shifting onto the siding, it was struck by the passenger train, travelling at top speed. Both trains were knocked off the tracks by the impact, with the passenger engine and cars actually flipping over. The passenger train's cars telescoped into each other, with the baggage car partially passing through one of the coaches, decapitating some of the passengers. Others were trapped alive in the wreckage, some dying of shock and exposure to the cold before they could be cut out of the crumpled cars.

The rescue effort began immediately. Passengers in the last cars were not badly injured and many of them quickly rushed out. They put out the fire by throwing snow on it, and worked with the conductor to set up a first aid station in two of the sleeper cars. Luckily, the crash's survivors included two doctors and three nurses, who immediately set to work treating the injured.

Twenty-six passengers and two crew members were killed. Another 32 people received serious injuries.

Newspaper journalists were soon on the scene to cover the story, where the wreck soon became a political matter between the Conservative *London Free Press* and the Liberal *London Advertiser*. The *Free Press* praised the Conservative government of the day for its foresight in building a new local hospital, which was used to treat the victims of the crash. The *Advertiser* slammed the *Free Press* as being the government's "pocket" organ.

The press also reported a shocking story that came out when the families of the crash victims were notified. It seems that one travelling salesman who had died in the collision had been secretly keeping two wives, one in Toronto and one in Hamilton.

An inquest into the disaster put most of the blame on Kerr's confusing message and on the engineer's interpretation of it. No charges were laid.

The Great Fire

April 19–20, 1904
Toronto

IN 1904, TORONTO WAS A BOOMING mid-sized city of 200,000 people, but many of its downtown office buildings lacked proper fire protection. Wooden beams, buildings built too close together, a lack of sprinkler systems and poorly protected electric and telephone wires all contributed to a dangerous situation.

At 8:04 on the very cold night of April 19, 1904, two simultaneous fire alarms rang out in Toronto's downtown core. Two night watchmen soon discovered flames coming out of the E.S. Currie Building at 58 Wellington Street W. and alerted the fire department. A team of firefighters arrived with Fire Chief John Thompson, but the fire was spreading so quickly that the building was already beyond hope.

The firefighters tried to contain the fire by breaking into the Gillespie-Ansley Building next door, but the flames quickly followed them and trapped them inside. It was only by sheer luck that the group escaped in time, by climbing down a rope from the third floor. Chief Thompson, among the men in the building, slipped while climbing the rope and broke his leg. Deputy Chief John Noble took over the rest of the operation.

At 8:51 PM, Noble sounded a general alarm to the city, letting everyone know that the fire was out of control. Every firefighter in Toronto was dispatched to fight the fire, and teams soon began arriving from other cities. By 11 PM, Hamilton's firefighters had arrived, and even the fire department from Buffalo, New York, showed up the next morning. By the time firefighters arrived from Brantford, Peterborough, London and Niagara Falls later the next day, it was clear that much of the city would be destroyed.

Firefighters had trouble not only with the fire but also with the high winds and freezing temperatures. Wind blew the water from their hoses back into their faces, freezing into ice. Indeed, the gusts were so strong that much of the water was blown across the street, hitting buildings on the opposite side.

The fire burned so hot, it was said, that nails were liquefied into molten metal.

At the *Evening Telegraph*, reporters had a story of their own to deal with. An office building across the street from them collapsed, setting their own Bay Street offices on fire. When the new sprinkler system failed to activate, and with firefighters preoccupied with other buildings, employees of the *Telegraph* were forced to fight the fire themselves. With wet paper towels over their faces and the help of a rooftop fire hydrant, they struggled for two hours before eventually putting out the fire—and earning a raise from the paper's publisher.

Firefighters fought the blaze in what at first seemed like a steadily losing battle. Live wires caught fire, sending sparks flying out of building windows. The temperatures stayed low, causing water from the hoses to continually freeze. The building facades soon became encrusted in ice, as did the firefighters' ladders.

Thousands of Toronto's citizens came out to watch the fire's progression. The mayor eventually conceded that some buildings might need to be destroyed to prevent the fire from spreading further. The army was called in to orchestrate the demolition, but because no dynamite could be found, the soldiers were deployed to control the crowds instead.

Flames soon spread to the opulent Queen's Hotel—the site of today's Royal York Hotel. Staff there had already evacuated all the guests and removed valuable items from the building. In an effort to slow the fire, the employees filled all the bathtubs with water and hung wet curtains over the windows. With the firefighters again preoccupied elsewhere, staff were forced to deal with the flames themselves and were able to extinguish the roof several times after it caught fire.

Eventually, the fire reached the Minerva Manufacturing Company's offices at Front and Yonge streets. The building had a firewall on its west side, and firefighters were able to stop the fire there and prevent its spread farther east. The fire came to a final halt after it burned the custom's house by the port. Firefighters knocked down the buildings surrounding it and thus were finally able to contain the Great Fire. Nonetheless, it continued to smoulder, and teams of firefighters had to watch the wreckage for two weeks afterwards to prevent any flare-ups and to cool the ruins.

Ontario's most destructive urban fire wiped out 7.7 hectares of Toronto's downtown core, gutting 98 buildings and destroying 137 businesses. The losses were estimated at the time as being worth $10.5 million. Overnight, 5000 people became jobless—though some found immediate work in the demolition and salvaging of the ruins.

Most of the city's financial core was destroyed, including many historic Georgian and Victorian shops and office buildings that would never be replaced, as well as some of the first skyscrapers. The core was quickly rebuilt, however, and the years that followed the fire saw some of Toronto's fastest vertical growth, and new, taller office

The smouldering ruins left behind by The Great Fire, which destroyed much of downtown Toronto in 1904.

towers in the gothic Chicago style became the norm of the city's skyline.

Miraculously, not a single person was killed by the fire. Few people lived in the downtown area of Toronto even then, and those who did were evacuated by the well-organized fire department. Only one death was indirectly blamed on the fire—demolition worker John Croft was killed two weeks after the fire when a dynamite charge blew up in his face. He had been working on the tear-down of the W.J. Gage Building on Front Street.

Spanish River Derailment

January 21, 1910
Spanish River

CANADIAN PACIFIC RAILWAY TRAIN #7 had left Sudbury at noon, with 100 passengers on board. It was headed for Minneapolis, pulling seven cars: a mail car, an express coach, a first-class coach, a diner coach, a sleeper coach and two second-class so-called "immigrant" coaches. These two cars contained most of the train's passengers, on their way from Europe to settle on the American or Canadian Prairies.

Once on board, the passengers immediately prepared for lunch. The travellers in second-class were expected to cook their own food, and the cars were outfitted with stoves for this purpose.

At 12:55 PM, the train began passing over a cantilever bridge at a speed of 75 kilometres per hour. Below, the frozen Spanish River stretched 80 metres wide and 9 metres deep.

"I felt the train pulling behind me in a very ragged manner, and I knew that the portion of the train behind me was off the track," baggage clerk William Dundas was quoted as saying. "For a distance the train pulled on; then I felt the air applied. I kept to the train when I felt her pulling up, and directly we were slowing down on the other side of the bridge; I jumped."

The first car containing the immigrants had derailed, but it still managed to be dragged across the bridge by the force of the engine. However, it also pulled the second immigrant car off the tracks. This car fared far worse. It came off the rails completely, slammed into a girder on the bridge and snapped in two. One half stayed on the bridge and caught on fire, while the other half fell over the edge, disappearing into a hole in the ice below. The first-class car dropped into the river as well, and the diner car rolled down the embankment, landing half-submerged. The sleeper car also rolled down but came to a rest on dry land.

Eight labourers working on the track nearby witnessed the horrendous disaster and rushed to help the wounded. The train's crew, now safely across the bridge on the engine, also ran back to help.

In all, 43 passengers died in the crash, and 38 were seriously injured. Most of the dead had been in the second immigrant car and in the first-class car.

P.D. James, a cigar salesman, was one of the few survivors from the first-class car. He had little memory of the crash but recalled a sudden feeling of falling, followed by all the lights on the car going out and water pouring in. James believed that the force of the crash had caused a movement of air pressure upwards, effectively shooting him out of the car to safety. He was found on the ice.

Another first-class passenger, B.J. Pearce, survived the partially submerged diner car by clinging onto a water cooler to keep afloat. Eventually he smashed through a ventilator to free himself from the car and swam to shore. Pearce and another passenger had drifted so far downstream by that point that they were no longer in sight of the crash. They walked to the village of Nairn Centre, where they were able to hop a freight train to the town of Nairn. It was only after getting there that they received medical attention and dry clothes.

Mrs. H.A. Linall of Winnipeg was considered a hero by many of the survivors of the crash. After bandaging her own head wound, she set up the sleeper car as a first aid station and treated other victims, wrapping their wounds with bedclothes and using whiskey as antiseptic. Linall reported treating many horribly wounded victims, including one who had been scalped by flying debris.

Conductor Thomas Reynolds, who was in the dining car at the time of the accident, barely survived. Still, he managed to save the lives of many others by helping them out of the freezing water and ice. Eventually, as the car began to be pulled further into the water by the current, he was forced to cut a hole with an axe to escape through, all the while helping more passengers get out. He was later awarded the Albert Medal for Lifesaving, at the time one of the most distinguished civil awards in the Commonwealth.

Local rescuers arrived within an hour, but damaged telegraph lines kept word from reaching Sudbury until much later. The first doctor arrived from the city five hours after the crash.

An inquest was held into the derailment on January 23, and a more formal coroner's inquest began two days later. Additionally, the Canadian Railway Commission conducted its own investigation. But for all this scrutiny, no conclusive explanations were drawn. The rails on the bridge were found to be warped and out of place, but it was unclear whether this had caused the derailment or if it had been the result of the derailment. When the cars were dredged out of the river, their wheels were too damaged for anything to be learned.

Parliament Hill Fire

February 3–4, 1916
Ottawa

AT ABOUT **8:50** PM ON FEBRUARY **3, 1916,** Francis Glass (Member of Parliament for Middlesex, East) was pouring over a newspaper in the parliamentary Reading Room. He reportedly felt a hot wind on his back and turned around to see the cause. Flames were coming out of the lower shelf of a nearby desk. This didn't come as much of a surprise—there had been 13 fires reported in the Parliament buildings between 1913 and 1916—but Glass rushed to get Constable Thomas S. Moore, who was posted to guard the Reading Room. Moore grabbed a fire extinguisher and tried to put out the fire, but the force of the blast from the extinguisher spread a stack of burning newspapers across the room. Within minutes, the room was engulfed in flames, and Glass and Moore ran for their lives.

At 8:57 PM, an automatic alarm alerted the firefighters from Number 8 fire station. They were on the scene by 9:00 PM, but within minutes the flames had spread across the House of Commons chamber and broken through the roof. The wood panelling inside the building kept the fire moving faster than it could be put out, and it quickly became apparent that the whole of Parliament would be destroyed.

"There is a big fire in the Reading Room, everyone get out quickly," shouted M.C.R. Steward, Chief Doorkeeper of the House of Commons, after bursting into the Chamber. (This was the last item recorded in Hansard, the official parliamentary minutes, for that day.) The members of parliament (who had been in the middle of a heated debate on how to market Canadian fish) and the speaker quickly bolted for the exits. Smoke soon began to pour into the room and MP William S. Loggie, who had been the last member to speak, had to be dragged out, semi-conscious, after inhaling the smoke.

Prime Minister Robert Borden was in his office when he was warned of the fire. Without grabbing his hat or coat, and with a handkerchief over his mouth, Borden quickly headed for the messenger's stairway, where he had to crawl down the stairs to stay below the smoke. In fact, the prime minister's office—built more recently than the rest of the building—was one of the few sections of the Parliament buildings not to burn. The prime minister's records (and his hat and coat) were salvaged, undamaged.

The firefighters, under Chief John W. Graham, struggled through the freezing cold night to prevent the fire from spreading to other buildings. A particular focus was put on the Parliamentary library, which contained all the government records. It was the quick thinking of a librarian, Connolly MacCormac, that saved the library. He closed the heavy metal doors that connected the library to the rest of the Parliament buildings, so preventing the spread of fire. Sir Sam Hughes, Minister of Militia and Defence, had been eating supper at the nearby Chateau Laurier when the fire broke out. He ordered the army onto the scene, and hundreds of soldiers joined in fighting the blaze and trying to rescue people and artifacts from the building.

In other parts of the building, various people had narrow escapes. Several in the Conservative Party offices on the second floor had to jump out the windows into the heavy snowbanks below, while others, trapped in a washroom, escaped by knotting towels together and climbing out the window. A certain M. Michel Siméon Delisle was reportedly getting a shave in the Parliamentary barber-shop. Despite smoke emanating from the ceiling, he ordered the barber to finish the shave—but when flames began coming out of the ceiling, the barber fled. Delisle himself barely escaped.

Seven people died in the fire, including one Member of Parliament, Bowman B. Law, from Nova Scotia. Law had been trapped and was almost completed burned by the fire—only a few bones were discovered between the House of Commons and the Reading Room. Prime Minister Borden later said of Bowman, "He was a man of kindly and generous disposition and indefatigable industry in connection with all his public duties. He was always listened to with attention and respect when he rose to address the House."

Two women who had been visiting friends in the building died when they chose to go back towards the fire to retrieve their furs. Strangely enough, two different men by the same name of Alphonse Desjardins—one a steamfitter and the other a police officer—died after a wall collapsed on them while they were fighting the fire.

Eventually the flames began to spread up the Victoria Tower, the highest point of the Parliament building (located where the Peace Tower stands today). The massive bell in the tower chimed nine, ten and eleven o'clock as the fire engulfed the building—but while tolling for midnight, the bell broke off and crashed down to the ground. At 12:30 AM, the clock stopped as well. By 1:21 AM, the celebrated widow's watch (called the "crown" because of its shape) collapsed in flames.

Water from the firefighters' hoses quickly froze on the building, covering it with a shiny, white coating. The statue of Sir John A. Macdonald was similarly caked. Despite the flying sparks all around them, firefighters managed to save the east and west block of Parliament, which was located a fair distance on each side of the main building.

Some paintings and furniture had been saved by people fleeing the building. These included a portrait of Queen Victoria, which had also been saved from the 1849 fire that destroyed earlier parliament buildings in Montréal. In each instance, the painting had to be cut out of its frame in order to fit through the doors.

However, the House of Commons mace—the symbol of Parliament's authority—could not be saved. It had been melted down into pools of gold and silver by the heat of the blaze. The metals were later reforged in England to construct a new mace, which was presented to the prime minister in 1917.

The hands of the old clock are now in the Bytown Museum, and the bell is preserved behind the new Parliament buildings as a memorial to the fire. In 1937, Prime Minister Mackenzie King built walls at his Kingsmere estate using bricks from the old Parliament.

The first cabinet meeting to discuss the situation took place at 11 PM on February 3—while the fire was still raging. It was decided to use the hall in the Victoria Memorial Museum (known today as the Canadian Museum of Nature) as a temporary House of Commons. The Senate was temporarily set up elsewhere in the museum, in a room that was reserved for extinct species and fossils—a "point which did not escape the notice of certain humourists," noted The Globe. On February 4, the day after the fire, Parliament was again in session.

An inquiry was immediately undertaken into the cause of the fire. Many people initially suspected some sort of German plot—as Canada was in the middle of World War I at the time. However, a Royal Commission into the fire

Firefighters hose down the icy remains of Canada's first parliament buildings. Only the parliamentary library (on the left) survived.

found no evidence of a plot, and witnesses reported no evidence of chemicals when the fire started (as would have occurred had some sort of accelerator been used).

Nevertheless, in the heat of the moment, a number of Germans (or suspected Germans) were rounded up. These included a man named Schuebier, who had stayed at the Chateau Laurier hotel but left in a rush. His interrogation revealed that his only crime was trying to skip out on a large hotel bill. Charles Strony, a pianist who had played at Rideau Hall the night before the fire, was also arrested—even though he was Belgian, not German. He was released after being held for three days. Montréal photographer Jules Verlier was arrested for photographing the fire—police suspected he might be a German agent—but he was released within an hour.

In the end, it was determined the fire must have been an accident, likely caused by a cigarette or cigar left in a wastepaper basket in the Reading Room. Smoking was forbidden in the building, but many MPs got away with it. No one came forward to admit to smoking in the Reading Room on the day of the fire.

Reconstruction of Parliament began immediately. When examining the ruins of the old building, architects determined that no portions of it—except the library wing, which had been unaffected—could be saved. It was a handsome structure, but it had been built cheaply, and numerous structural problems had cropped up, even before the fire. Plus, the government wanted another floor added, which the old foundations and walls could not support.

The building was completely torn down and rebuilt, albeit in a similar style as the original. Only the tower was dramatically different. The old, German-styled Victoria Tower was replaced by the more austere Peace Tower. Parliament members moved into the new building in 1920, but it was not until 1927—the 60th anniversary of Confederation—that the tower was completed.

Munitions Plant Explosion

❖

October 14–15, 1918
Trenton

IT WAS A DIFFICULT TIME. With both Canada and Britain in the thick of World War I, few skilled workers could be found to take industrial jobs. Still, British Explosives Limited managed to attract 2500 workers to their massive industrial plant. The factory was built in 1916 just outside the small city of Trenton, on the shore of Lake Ontario. It specialized in explosives of all kinds, including TNT, gun cotton and black powder.

The location was important to the British-based company. Canadian Forces Base (CFB) Trenton was the mustering and training grounds for tens of thousands of Canadian soldiers destined for Europe. Even today, CFB Trenton remains one of the most important army bases in Canada.

On October 14, 1918, the war was nearing its end. Although no one knew it at the time, Germany would agree to an armistice on November 11—less than a month away. Explosives and guns were being pumped out of the factory in record numbers, arming successive waves of young men headed for the trenches of Europe.

In the evening of October 14, an acid tank in the factory overflowed before employees could control it, starting a fire. At 7:10 PM, the fire spread to the TNT warehouses, and the first explosion occurred. It shook the plant with such a force that many believed it was an earthquake. The fire continued to spread and catch on to other buildings. Between 12 and 14 explosions were reported before 6:30 the next morning. Over the course of the night, fully half of the plant had been wiped out.

The main buildings within the compound—the TNT and gun cotton plants—were immediately levelled. However, some 100 smaller outer buildings survived. Through careful work, firefighters were able to keep the blaze away from the nitric acid tanks and sulphuric gas chambers. Had the fire reached these parts of the plant, the disaster would have been incalculably greater and might well have killed thousands of people.

Fearing for the worst, many residents of Trenton evacuated the city and headed for nearby Brighton. Others— especially those with family or friends in the plant—rushed towards the fire to see what was happening. Buildings were shaken and the explosions could be heard as far away as Belleville, 15 kilometres east.

It was said that every window in Trenton was smashed—the damage from broken glass alone was estimated at $25,000. Power lines were also knocked over by the force of the explosions, leaving the city in the dark. However, because the plant was located 3 kilometres outside of the city, and separated from it by a hill, Trenton was spared any serious destruction.

Only one factory worker was killed in the explosion, though many others were injured, mainly from the flying shards of glass. When the war's end came a few weeks later, it was clear that there would be no purpose in rebuilding the plant, and its remains were abandoned.

Trans-Canada Airlines Crash

ON THE EARLY MORNING OF FEBRUARY 6, 1941, a plane crashed near the remote town of Armstrong, north of Thunder Bay. The small Trans-Canada Airlines passenger flight had started in Montréal, with earlier stops in Ottawa and Toronto. In addition to the passengers, it carried a shipment of express mail. Its final destination was to be Winnipeg, over 600 kilometres to the west.

But heavy snowstorms forced the pilot to change his route sharply. He had already passed Armstrong when he became concerned about fuel supplies and decided to head back to make an unscheduled landing at the town's airstrip. Radio communication was made with the Winnipeg airport to inquire about the weather there. The final radio message by the plane's pilot, at 4:47 AM, reported that all was well. Ground grew at Armstrong started to prepare for the plane's landing—a landing that never came.

When it was clear that something tragic had happened to the aircraft, search crews were immediately sent out into the dense forest south of Armstrong to investigate. The journey proved slow and arduous, with heavy snow and high winds hampering the trek through the woods. The only road heading south of the town was buried under 3 metres of snow.

Eventually, the wreckage of the plane was located 1.5 kilometres south of Armstrong. The doomed aircraft had hit the tops of the trees and flipped over, tearing itself to shreds. All 12 people on board—nine passengers and three crew—were found dead.

Unusually, no fire or explosion had occurred. The pilot appeared to have cut the ignition, suggesting that he knew a crash was about to happen. The cargo of mail was salvaged, unharmed, to be sent on to Winnipeg.

An inquiry into the cause of the crash proved inconclusive. The plane's wings showed no sign of icing, no mechanical problems were found with the plane and a test of the pilot's blood showed no evidence of alcohol or carbon monoxide poisoning.

The supervising coroner, Dr. S. Lawson, did point a finger at Emil Kading, one of the air engineers at the Armstrong airport who was in charge of arranging landings and refueling. A German citizen and "enemy alien" during World War II, Kading was thought to have carried out some sort of sabotage. However, further investigation showed that he did not have any impact on the crash.

The Trans-Canada Airlines crash was the company's worst since it had initiated passenger flights in 1938. It was also the worst air disaster in Canada at the time, though it was quickly overshadowed by the American Airlines crash near St. Thomas. It remains one of the country's greatest aviation mysteries.

American Airlines DC-3 Crash

October 30, 1941
St. Thomas

THE CRASH OF THE AMERICAN AIRLINES DC-3 near St. Thomas, Ontario, was the stuff of nightmares for local children.

"For months after the crash, when in bed at night, if I heard a plane coming I shut my eyes tightly and plugged my ears, expecting either to be bombed or the plane to crash," said Beth Vicary, who had lived 10 kilometres south of the crash site. "I never told my parents how scared I was."

"We parked the car and as we approached the burning wreck, I saw a human foot hanging on a wire fence alongside the road, and a blackened form that my father told me was the body of the stewardess, Mary Blackley, who had been thrown from the aircraft when it hit the ground." said Jim Johnston, who was 10 at the time.

The bodies of the dead were so badly pulverized that George Lumley, the owner of the general store in the nearby village of Iona, donated his shoe boxes to collect the remains.

There were no survivors. Seventeen passengers and three crew members died, making it the worst air disaster at that time in Canada.

The *St. Thomas Times-Journal* reported that the plane had been flown by an experienced pilot—34-year-old David I. Cooper of Plandome, New York. The regional American flight was on route from Detroit to Buffalo. Just minutes before the crash, while passing over the town of

Jarvis at 9:30 PM, Cooper radioed ahead to Buffalo to say that everything was all right. However, when the airplane passed over the village of Lawrence Station, near St. Thomas, it began circling dangerously. After circling several times in a 5-kilometre circumference and dropping lower and lower, a bright light shot out of the aircraft. Eyewitnesses thought it was a flare to help the pilot find a place to land in the darkness.

"The plane moved closer to the ground, shot quickly upwards and then just as suddenly crashed. There was a great explosion as the ship rammed its nose into the ground and flames roared into the night," the *Times-Journal* continued.

The plane came to rest in an oat field on the Howe farm property, outside of St. Thomas. Thompson Howe was the first person to see the crash and ran to the site from his farmhouse, which was half a kilometre away. A number of others who had watched the circling plane quickly arrived on the scene, including provincial police, neighbours and officers from the nearby Royal Canadian Air Force training school in Fingal.

A crew of firefighters arrived from Shedden. And even with scores of volunteers carrying water from Howe's well, it took two hours before the fire could be brought under control.

The body of Cooper, the pilot, was found badly burned in the cockpit, still holding the control lever, which had broken off.

The plane had crashed while on course, and it was thought that the heavy fog that night had made impossible what might have been an emergency landing attempt. However, the initial cause of the disaster, which necessitated the landing, remains a mystery.

Sinking of the *Wawinet*

September 21, 1942
Georgian Bay (Lake Huron)

UNLIKE MOST OF THE OTHER SERIOUS SHIPWRECKS of the Great Lakes—which typically were industrial or large passengers ships—the *Wawinet* was a small pleasurecraft. Today, its loss still holds the record for the worst noncommercial disaster in Georgian Bay.

Wawinet's owner was the former NHL player Bertrand "Bert" Corbeau. Corbeau was a native of Penetanguishene and had played for the Montréal Canadiens, Toronto Maple Leafs, the Toronto St. Patricks (the predecessors of the Maple Leafs) and the now-defunct Hamilton Tigers. In 1916, his first year as a professional player, Corbeau's team, the Canadiens, won the Stanley Cup. In 1924, he was one of the leading scorers in the NHL. He also had a reputation as a tough guy—in 1921, 1924 and 1926 he led the league in penalty minutes. After retiring as a player, Corbeau coached several minor league teams and eventually accepted a position as manager of the Midland Foundry and Machine Co.

It was in the midst of World War II that the company was producing metal parts for armaments. They had just finished a major contract earlier than expected, and Corbeau kindly invited his employees out on a fishing trip to celebrate. Of the 45 men employed by the company, 41 decided to go on the trip.

September 21, 1942, seemed like the perfect evening for such a cruise. The weather was exceptionally warm for late September; the sky was blue and the lake was calm.

The men could relax, fish over the side of the ship and enjoy plenty of cold drinks with the beautiful Thirty Thousand Islands scenery.

The steel propeller yacht left Penetanguishene at 4 PM, with Corbeau at the controls. The group made their way up to Honey Harbour, where they stopped at the Delawana Inn to pick up drinks and food. After that, the *Wawinet* started its journey back to Penetanguishene. Late that evening at 10 PM, the boat was passing Beausoleil Island when it struck a sandbar.

What immediately followed is unclear—other than the boat slipped under the perfectly calm waters within two minutes. Twenty-five men—as well as Corbeau—lost their lives. Only 17 survived by swimming to Beausoleil Island, nearby.

The survivors spent the night huddled in a remote cabin on the island, watching as the bodies of their coworkers washed up on shore. When the alarm was sounded, dozens of boats from Midland and Penetanguishene sailed up to rescue the men and to search for more survivors. None were found.

An inquest into the sinking of the *Wawinet* proved inconclusive. The men's recollection of the night was clouded with alcohol (it seemed that a lot more drinking than fishing had been going on). Corbeau had run the *Wawinet* into a sandbar in an area he knew like the back of his hand, having sailed there constantly since childhood. Had he been drinking so heavily that he had lost track of the boat's position?

The list of victims and survivors seemed random. Some of the strongest swimmers among the men had drowned, while others who couldn't swim at all had easily made it to safety.

As always, fate would cause many ironies. Some men had not been so keen to go on the trip but had been encouraged by friends and family. A few would gladly have went but missed out for some reason or another. Mr. Carruthers of Wyebridge had desperately raced to the dock in a cab, only to see the *Wawinet* leaving for Honey Harbour without him. The future mayor of Penetanguishene, Gilbert Robilliard, reported that his father had been one of the few company employees not to go on the trip, since he had other work to do that night.

A few men jumped off the side of the ship opposite Beausoleil Island. In the confusion and dark they tried to head for the first piece of land they saw, which was Present Island, much farther away than Beausoleil. Some made it, but most did not.

Stewart Cheetham, who escaped to Present Island, described his experience.

> *I was on the boat when it suddenly swerved and soon started to sink. I jumped into the water and in the moonlight could see an island ahead of me. The water was much warmer than the air and was calm, so I knew I could make it if I took my time and didn't get excited. I finally reached the shore and then made my way to the end of the island where I knew there was a guard's cabin. I found it and woke him up and later he took me across to Beausoleil, where I joined the other sixteen. I did not see or hear any of the others from the time I started swimming.*

For unknown reasons, the *Wawinet*'s ballast had been removed shortly before the trip. Had Corbeau done this to make the boat go faster? The lack of ballast would certainly have made the ship unstable and top-heavy, and it could have caused the ship to tip over after hitting the shoal.

It was common knowledge that Corbeau enjoyed shocking his passengers by rocking the boat wildly back and forth. Had he tried this again and gone too far? In addition, the portholes—which Corbeau had recently redesigned to be rectangular instead of circular—had been left open. Rocking, or the force of hitting the shoal, would have quickly filled the boat with water.

The loss of wage earners devastated the families of the men who drowned. At the time, Penetanguishene was still coming out of the Depression, and few had any savings to draw on.

Kam Kotia Mine Pollution

IN 1943, THE CANADIAN GOVERNMENT faced a serious shortage of raw materials. Feeding the massive demand for tanks, ships, aircraft, guns and bombs for the war—as well as other wartime necessities—had depleted the country's supply of a number of metals. With the United States' entry into World War II in 1941, the American Metal Reserves and Wartimes Supplies Board put increasing pressure on the Canadian government to assist their country with raw materials.

To solve this crisis, a crown agency known as the Wartime Metals Corporation was created, and it was tasked with opening new mines and processing plants.

An area 35 kilometres northwest of Timmins was selected as a site for a new copper mine. Known as the Kam Kotia mine, it was located near the scenic Lake Kamiskota and the Kamiskota River.

The Wartime Metals Corporation created the company Kam Kotia Mines Ltd. Under special powers afforded to the government during the war, it was able to order Hollinger Mining—a local company that specialized in gold mining—to operate Kam Kotia Mines. The Wartime Metals Corporation paid for all the mine's operating costs and offered Hollinger royalties on the copper it produced.

The mine operated for only a little over a year, from September 1943 to December 1944. A total of 25,000 tonnes of copper were produced for the war effort, at a loss of $140,223. By late 1944, a number of new copper

mines had opened in the U.S., and the American government was no longer pressuring Canada for a supply of the
metal, so the mine was closed.

However, during this brief period, it managed to
became what was—and still is—the greatest environmental disaster related to mining in Ontario. Over 60
years later, it is surrounded by an area of 500 hectares
that is unable to support virtually any form of life.

In their rush to produce copper, Hollinger left behind
tremendous amounts of "tailings," or leftover materials
from mining. The oxidization of the sulphate in their tailings caused acidic runoff into surrounding watersheds.
Pollution spread into nearby lakes and streams, including
Lake Kamiskota—a favourite cottage destination for residents of Timmins. Eventually, the pollution was carried
north into Hudson Bay.

In 1973, Hollinger when bankrupt, and its assets—
including Kam Kotia Mines Ltd.—reverted to the provincial
government.

The environmental group MiningWatch, in describing
the area's appearance today, states "Dead trees sticking
out of the swamp and rotting vegetation create a scene
from a Hollywood horror movie." In 2002, the provincial
environmental commissioner Gordon Miller visited the
remote site and was equally shocked, saying "This is
the worst case of all our mine rehabilitations in the province. It's the biggest mess and is the highest priority of our
department."

There are currently 200,000 tonnes of waste rock and
6 million tonnes of tailings on the site. Although these
have now been treated, the pollution already has grown
so extensive that it is estimated the cleanup will cost
between $28 and $40 million. The cleanup would include
building a dam to stop the pollution from spreading farther,

removing all the tailings within the dam area, treating all the area's water and physically converting the mine itself.

It was not until 1999—after decades of complaints from local residents and cottagers—that the provincial government began the process to clean up the pollution. So far, a water pumping and treatment system has been built, which must pump out all the water in a 48-hectare area. As of 2003, the provincial government announced that it would invest $60 million in its Abandoned Mines Rehabilitation Project. Premier Dalton McGuinty specifically named Kam Kotia as a major recipient of some of that funding. At present, the cleanup is slowly underway.

Noronic Fire

THE EARLY 20TH CENTURY WAS THE GOLDEN AGE of ocean-liner travel. Huge ships vied for the position of largest and most opulent, with names such as *Mauritania, Olympic, Britannic, Normandie, Queen Mary* and *Imperator.* Some of them met tragic ends, and their names—*Titanic, Empress of Ireland* and *Lusitania*—became synonymous with disaster.

Passenger ships on the Great Lakes had their own competition for greatness, albeit on a more modest scale. Among the biggest names was the *Noronic,* laid down in 1913, in Port Arthur (now Thunder Bay), Ontario, at a cost of $3.5 million. She could hold up to 600 passengers and 200 crew, was 110 metres in length and weighed 6400 tonnes. Along with her sister ships *Huronic* and *Harmonic, Noronic* was the largest ship on the lakes, earning the nickname "Queen of the Great Lakes." She usually sailed with a full musical band on board, and as well as ferrying passengers between the great port cities of the lakes, hosted opulent parties and events. Originally owned by Northern Navigation Lines, the ship was later bought by Canada Steamship Lines.

In 1949, *Noronic* was middle aged but still the biggest. Although road and air travel had overtaken ships as the fastest way to move around the lakes, there was still a niche for high-end tourist travel.

On September 14, the ship left Detroit for a weeklong tour of Lake Erie and Lake Ontario, arriving in Toronto on the 17th. The 525 passengers on board were mostly

American tourists. While anchored in Toronto Harbour, the ship's crew became complacent. Captain William Taylor was dining with friends off the boat, and First Officer Gerald Wood had been left in charge until midnight. The wheelhouse—which was supposed to be guarded at all times—was left empty for long periods of time. Two officers were assigned to fire patrol duty, but for some reason, their assignment ended at midnight.

At 2:30 AM, one of the passengers, a fire insurance specialist named Don Church, began to smell smoke. On closer investigation, he found smoke coming out of one of the linen rooms and heard the sounds of someone trapped inside it. Church rushed to get a nearby bellhop, Ernest O'Neill, to open the door.

As soon as the door was opened, the rush of oxygen caused the small fire to grow quickly. Church and O'Neill tried to use fire extinguishers to put out the blaze, but it did little to tame the fire. Then the men tried to use the firehoses but found that they had not been maintained and were out of order. O'Neill went to alert First Officer Wood, who tried to sound the klaxon horns in the wheelhouse to request help from Toronto. Unfortunately, the horns jammed, producing almost no sound.

Very little bravery was seen on board the ship. Many crew members had been tasked to man fire extinguishers in the case of an emergency, but being unable to make it to their stations, they simply abandoned ship. O'Neill himself later testified that although he had alerted some passengers about the danger while he tried to put out the fire, evacuating everyone on the ship had never crossed his mind. Passengers began a frenzied rush to escape the burning ship, climbing over top of one another and even crushing one woman to death.

By 2:44 AM—only 14 minutes after the fire started—
Toronto's fire chief arrived at the docks. The ship was so
badly burned already that he was surprised that anyone
could still be alive. In fact, many passengers had made it
to the starboard side, where they were now stuck. Their
choice was either jumping several stories into the cold
water below, or burning on the ship. Not surprisingly,
most jumped. On the port side, facing the docks, fire
crews assembled ladders to let the passengers climb down.
In some cases, firefighters actually climbed onto the
burning ship to rescue passengers.

Eleven-year-old passenger Kathleen Kerr tried to climb
down to the dock along a steel cable, burning her hands
and feet on the hot metal. Another passenger climbing
down the same cable knocked the girl off, sending her
hurtling down into the water 10 metres below. Luckily,
she was able to swim to shore. A stranger saved Kerr's six-
year-old sister by carrying her down the cable on his back.
The girls' brother and parents never made it off the
Noronic.

Several passersby were able to do tremendous work
rescuing the passengers who had jumped into the water.
Ross Leitch used his water taxi to bring many people to
shore, sometimes having to dodge other falling passengers as they jumped off the deck. Another man, Donald
Williamson, was standing by the docks when the ship
caught fire. He managed to commandeer a nearby raft
and used it to ferry some 20 people to safety.

One of the men rescued was Captain Taylor, who had
returned to the ship when the fire started. The ladder he
was climbing down broke and he fell into the water. Firefighters had to dive into the water to rescue him again.

Many passengers had been drinking heavily earlier
that night, making rescue difficult. A few were too ine-
briated to even understand what was going on. One man

The burnt interior of the luxury passenger ship, *Noronic*. A fire destroyed the *Noronic* while it was anchored in Toronto Harbour in 1949, claiming 118 lives.

~ගිC~

who had jumped in the water refused to get out because he had lost his pyjama pants.

Two police officers, Detective Cyril Cole and Constable Robert Anderson, dove into the harbour and managed to save most of the victims in the water. Indeed, after a thorough search of the harbour the day after the fire, only one body was found in the water. However, 119 passengers—including one Canadian—had perished on board the ship. The entire crew escaped.

The fire was followed by massive public outrage—from the survivors, the families of the victims and the general population of Toronto. Captain Taylor, intoxicated at the time of the fire, was hauled into a Toronto court. He had his licence suspended for one year and never again captained a vessel.

A House of Commons inquiry into the fire blamed its cause on a number of factors, which included ineptitude and cowardice of the crew, who had little training in fire prevention; the improperly maintained water hoses; and the highly flammable oiled wood panelling that filled the interior of the ship. Canada Steamship Lines was ordered to pay $2 million to the families of the deceased and to cover the costs of the inquiry.

The ship itself had partially sunk by the time the fire was put out. Salvage crews later were able to force air into the wreck in order to bring it up to the surface. It was then towed to Hamilton, where it was broken up for scrap.

In 1981, the future Prime Minister Paul Martin purchased Canada Steamship Lines, and it is now one of the world's largest cargo shipping companies. It no longer runs passenger ships. As for the *Noronic*, the only piece of it remaining is its whistle, displayed in the nautical collection at Toronto's Harbourfront.

Coniston Bus-Train Crash

February 9, 1951
Coniston (near Sudbury)

LIKE SO MANY OTHER DISASTERS, this one started as a series of problems that seemed to be asking for trouble.

In the deathly cold of a northern Ontario winter, a Coniston bus approached a railway crossing, which had no signals. The temperature had dropped to almost -45°C, and the bus was crowded; due to the cold weather, more commuters had crammed in than usual. Instead of its maximum capacity of 32, 45 people were on board the bus on the morning of February 9, 1951. The bus' windshield was heavily fogged and its windows were caked with ice and frost.

Then, just as the bus was passing over the tracks, it was struck on the side by the "Dominion Flyer," a Canadian Pacific passenger train on its way from Montréal to Sudbury. The force threw the bus 25 metres through the air. Some passengers, thrown through the windows, landed as far as 60 metres from the crossing.

"There was a great dull thud," local barber Arthur Dumont told the *Globe and Mail*. He had been taking out the ashes from the woodstove of his nearby shop, and "I looked up to see the end of the bus whirl down the track through the air. The driver was crawling out the window when I got there. Inside, people were screaming to be let out."

Dumont rushed to the bus and began pulling victims out of the wreckage, with the help of other neighbours. "I felt something beneath my foot in the snow. It was a man's face. He was unconscious. Then he began to scream. We carried him to the train."

A woman who lived nearby, Mrs. Bukacheski, went to the scene to help with first aid. "She came up to see the two women I carried into my barber shop," said Dumont. "She gave them sedatives and accompanied them when they were carried to the train. She did a wonderful job and never lost her nerve in the turmoil."

Sleeping car number 27 became a makeshift hospital as doctors arrived on the scene. It took an hour and a half to extract the dead and wounded from the wreck.

Many of the people on the bus had been workers coming off the night shift at the smelting plant. At the time, Coniston was a company town, owned by a mining and smelting company. Other passengers included women on their way from Coniston to Sudbury for shopping, as well as young girls on their way to school.

In total, five bus passengers were killed, along with two passengers on the train.

Bus driver Edward Carriere was adamant that the accident was not his fault. "I feel terrible about this, but it was an accident I can't accept responsibility for," he told the *Globe and Mail*. "A wigwag should be placed at that crossing. Even in good visibility there is a spur line which usually has coal cars on it and the view is completely blocked."

An intense debate began over the series of events that had led up to the crash. Carriere—who was charged with manslaughter—insisted that he had stopped at the tracks but had been unable to see the train because of the weather conditions. He also said that the train had not blown its whistle in warning. The train's engineer testified that he had blown his whistle and that he had heard the crossing siren going off as well. However, nearby witnesses testified that the bus had not stopped, nor had there been any whistle or siren!

Williamsburg Canal Bus Crash

July 31, 1953
Near Morrisburg (Stomont, Dundas and Glengarry County)

A TORONTO-MONTRÉAL EXPRESS BUS was travelling east along the old Highway 2 on the night of July 31, 1953. In order to keep on schedule, the driver was going over the speed limit. The bus was passing the small town of Morrisburg, some 50 kilometres west of Cornwall, when it hit the back of a stalled truck.

The truck's lights had been off, and in the dark, the bus driver had no hope of seeing the truck until it was too late. Indeed, two other trucks had gone into the ditch earlier that night, trying to avoid one that was parked in the middle of the highway. One of the other truck drivers had notified the Ontario Provincial Police. As it turned out, a constable was already on his way to investigate when the bus appeared on the scene.

The fateful location of the crash prevented it from being a routine highway collision. The accident took place at the exact point where Highway 2 passed the Williamsburg Canal, a part of the larger Morrisburg Canal.

The impact of the crash knocked the bus off the road and into the waters of the canal, where it quickly became totally submerged. The vehicle was badly damaged, partly by an explosion in the engine that had occurred on impact. When the police arrived, work immediately began to rescue the passengers and haul the bus out of the canal. With the use of tractors, it took two hours to bring the wreck back onto the road.

By that point, 20 of the bus' 37 passengers had already drowned. Of the dead, 10 were still on the bus when it was pulled out of the water. The survivors, with the help of rescuers, had managed to swim to the shore.

"The first thing I remembered was an explosion followed by what looked like a blue flash," Ronald Mortishead from Ireland told the Globe and Mail. "Then the bus seemed to be turning over and over. I don't know whether it did or not, but that was my impression."

Mortishead soon realized that the bus was filling with water. He could hear others, trapped in the wreckage, calling out for help. "A fellow behind me pulled himself up on the luggage rack and shoved his feet through the window. He went through first and I followed him. My head was practically under water before I got out, and just after that the bus filled completely with water."

Some of the passengers who made it to shore in good health were quick to go back and work to rescue others. One of those, 23-year-old John Fanya, tragically drowned after rescuing four people.

Claude Desjardins, a passenger from Québec City, thought that panic had ruined others' chances of survival. "They were screaming so much they lost their strength. Many of them were terror stricken and didn't know what to do."

"I must have banged my head when the bus went over the edge," said Carson Allen of Nova Scotia

> I wasn't out, but when the shock wore off, all the people around me were gone. The sailor sitting next to me must have got out somehow or other. The water was pouring in and the bus was tipping on my side. I went over to the other side and broke the glass with my fist. As I got out, the bus gave a last roll, and sank. I must have been one of the last to get out and people were still

*screaming in the coach. As I reached the bank and
looked back, the lights of the bus shone up eerily out of
the water. It was unbelievable that in such a short time
so much had happened.*

In the end, both drivers survived the accident
unharmed, though they had to be treated for shock.
The driver of the stalled truck, Max Roodman, and the
bus driver, Lorne Chesbrough, were both charged with
manslaughter for their reckless behaviour. Chesbrough's
charge was later changed to dangerous driving.

Today, there is no evidence of the site where the bus
plunged into the Williamsburg Canal. In fact, the canal
no longer exists. With the formation of the St. Lawrence
Seaway in 1958, the area was flooded and submerged
under water. Highway 2 was rerouted and replaced by
Highway 401, the major route between Toronto and
Montréal.

RCAF Crash into Convent

＊

May 15, 1956
Orléans (Carleton County)

ONE OF ONTARIO'S MOST FREAKISH ACCIDENTS occurred on May 15, 1956, when an RCAF CF-100 jet slammed into a convent near Ottawa.

The mysterious crash started with a sighting of an unidentified aircraft. With the Cold War at its height, the Canadian airforce was perpetually on high alert. They sent up a CF-100 Interceptor to investigate. At 9:30 PM, the airforce plane radioed back to its base to announce that the mystery plane was in fact a civilian "friendly" craft.

With their investigation completed, the CF-100 began taking part in some practice interception manoeuvres, but bad weather had crept over the sky. It was foggy and overcast, and weather reports had forecast hail.

Without radioing the base again, the CF-100 suddenly plummeted 10,000 metres out of the sky, and at 10:17 PM hit the Villa Saint Louis, a residence for elderly nuns. The aircraft was travelling well over 1000 kilometres per hour at the time.

Unconfirmed reports from the owner of a nearby restaurant said that the plane had been on fire before hitting the ground.

The crash was bizarre not only because of the jet's drop from the sky but also because it hit the convent so directly. The Villa Saint Louis was situated in the middle of an open field. It was the only structure within kilometres.

An RCAF officer later described the likelihood of hitting the convent as "1000 to 1." It could only be described as intensely bad luck.

William Schmidt and Kenneth Thomas, the two airmen aboard the CF-100, died on impact. A massive explosion was set off at the convent, and a fire broke out. Residents of Orléans who had heard the crash drove to the scene to see what they could do. Vern Ayrhart, Lorne Barber and John Crete were the first to arrive at Villa Saint Louis and quickly began to rescue the elderly women from the burning building.

"I can hear the screams yet," Ayrhart later told the *Globe and Mail*.

"I heard others banging on the walls inside, but I was forced back from the fire escape by the heat," said Barber.

Gloria Flora, aged 14, arrived at the fire with her parents. "Mommy and I stood there and cried," she said. "I was sick to my stomach when the screams died off. I knew what that meant. Mommy and I went back inside and beside our beds and prayed for our friends."

"It was horrible," said Sister Louise Auguste, who had survived the crash. "The whole building seemed to burst into flames at once. I think everyone on the top floor must have been burned. Many on the ground floor were also unable to get out. The plane made a terrific crash when it hit. At first I thought it was a bomb."

A total of 35 elderly nuns were in the building at the time. Since it was their routine to go to bed at 8 PM, they were already asleep at the time of the crash. Many were in frail health to begin with, and 20 had recently undergone operations. A number of the women were trapped because they were too weak to break through the mosquito screens covering the windows.

The brick and stone building was only two years old at the time, but it soon became clear that the fire had grown too great and none of it could be saved.

"An old nun jumped into my arms," said rescuer Ray Rainville to *The Globe*. "I had just finished on the other side when I heard yelling and I ran over there. I yelled to a nun there to break the window. Don't ask me how she did it, but she landed in my arms and I went down with her."

Survivors were rushed to Ottawa General Hospital, many in only their nightgowns. One woman lost all her hair to the flames.

One priest, Reverend Richard Ward, was at Villa Saint Louis at the time. He was thrown nearly 50 metres across the lawn by the force of the explosion.

"My brother, Joe, another brother, Lucien, and I picked up the priest," said Wilfred Potvin. "He was still living. We listened to his heart and it was still beating, but very faintly. He died about 10 minutes later."

Fifteen people were killed in the disaster, including 11 nuns and a cook who had been employed at the convent.

Defence Minister Ralph Campney apologized for the disaster on behalf of the government.

Despite his best endeavours and the ingenuity of modern science, man's mastery of machines can never be complete. It is a cause for profound sorrow that this accident has taken the lives of so many selfless members of the religious vocation and two members of a service whose mission it is to do everything within its power, by day and night, to provide security for the Canadian way of life.

An investigation into the crash found no conclusive explanations for its cause. The mostly likely cause was said to have been a malfunction in the CF-100's oxygen system, causing the crew members to lose control of the plane and black out.

The Villa Saint Louis was rebuilt in 1965, and it remains a home for elderly nuns today. On May 14, 2006, the 50th anniversary of the disastrous crash was commemorated. A cross, 6 metres high, was put up at the crash site. It is surrounded by stones taken from the original convent.

Gas Explosion at Metropolitan Store

❦

October 25, 1960
Windsor

ON OCTOBER 25, 1960, Windsor's Metropolitan Department Store was rocked by a sudden explosion that destroyed most of the building.

The Metropolitan was a large store, selling everything from clothing to hardware to furniture. The afternoon had been a relatively quiet one, with 80 employees on duty. About 100 customers were in the store. At the top of the basement stairway, manager Joseph Halford was looking down, watching workers install a new gas furnace. The installation finished, workers were filling the boiler with water and bleeding air from a pipe that led to the 12-centimetre gas main.

Suddenly, just after 3 PM, there was a tremendous explosion. "All at once the roof fell in, I guess," Halford later told the *Globe and Mail*. "The lights went out. There was dust everywhere and I saw daylight through a small hole in the collapsed wall."

A fire quickly broke out at the back of the store, but Halford was able to escape before the heat and smoke became too severe. He had not smelled any gas just before the explosion, though he later guessed that there must have been a gas leak that was ignited by the water heater.

Up and down Ouellette Avenue, the damage was great. The entire back of the store had collapsed into rubble.

Six cars parked in the back alley were destroyed. The basement stairway was filled with debris, trapping all those who were below.

The front of the building withstood the explosion, but there was still huge amounts of damage, including piles of broken glass and twisted metal. Pedestrians and drivers on Ouellette Avenue were injured by the flying debris. Heaps of toys, clothing, hardware and mannequins—as well as human victims—filled the street. Determining the death counts was initially confusing because the mannequins, partly obscured under rubble, were often mistaken for people.

There was a moment of shocked silence following the explosion. Then cries for help could be heard. These cries went on for over two hours.

"People were strewn all over the street, some screaming and covered with blood," reported passerby Lou Hulay. "The store, it was dark and filled with smoke. Screams filled the air and you couldn't see the victims…. It was the worst thing I've ever seen. People were under piles of brick, cement and steel. Only the legs of some were visible."

"I saw two women tossed into the street like dolls," said Helen Stanton, who had been entering the store at the time of the explosion. "They hurtled right out of the store just like that. It was awful."

"God was good to me," said store clerk Irene Lennox. "I had been serving a customer at my counter in the basement and had gone upstairs to help her to her car with an armful of goods. If it had not been for that, I'd probably be dead now. I heard a tremendous bang. The next minute I was on the street, 30 feet away." Lennox was lucky enough to escape with no physical injuries.

"There was an explosion. The next thing I was flying through the air," said 17-year-old soda fountain clerk Janet Lesperence. "Then I only saw stars. I think I was unconscious about 20 minutes. Several other children were crying and women were screaming. I was pinned to the floor by the bar across my stomach. My head was pinned sideways by some debris. I could only move my arms and I waved my hands to attract rescuers. I thought I was paralyzed from the waist down. I couldn't feel my legs. When the bar was lifted I could walk, though."

"We came here to make a new life. Why did this have to happen?" cried Michael Zack when he learned that his wife had died. He had been with his son in the hospital when the explosion occurred. Both Zack and his wife were Polish Jews who had survived the Holocaust, in which they lost their parents.

Ten people were killed in the explosion and 90 injured. It remains the worst commercial workplace disaster in Ontario's history. Damages to the building and its contents were pegged at $500,000.

It was considered lucky that the offices in the floor above the store—ironically, belonging to an insurance company—were largely spared from the blast. Those working upstairs were all able to escape with their lives.

Although it is difficult, it is sometimes necessary to find humour in horrific situations. A photographer on the scene after the explosion discovered two goldfish in the building. Apparently they had been blown out of a fish tank as it shattered and had landed safely in a small pot from the cookware department. Enough water from the fish tank had somehow made it into the cup that the fish were sustained. Apart from a few missing scales, the pair were unharmed; they were swimming between lumps of plaster and shards of broken glass. The photographer named the fish "Lucky George" and "Hell's Belle."

Grassy Narrows Mercury Poisoning

1962–1970 (and beyond)
Grassy Narrows, or Asubpeeschoseewagong (Kenora District)

MERCURY WAS USED BY DRYDEN CHEMICALS in the process of bleaching paper. Between 1962 and 1970, the pulp and paper mill dumped some 9000 kilograms of mercury into the Wabigoon River. In 1970, the provincial government ordered the plant to stop this practice, but the damage had already been done. Five hundred kilometres of river were poisoned, starting from the Wabigoon and leading to the English River, and eventually crossing the Manitoba border into Lake Winnipeg.

The result has been an almost unparellelled environmental and human catastrophe, possibly the worst in Ontario's history.

"One day [in May 1970] government people just came and told us to stop fishing," a member of the Grassy Narrows First Nation told American author Anastasia Shkilnyk. She published her findings in the book, *A Poison Stronger than Love: The Destruction of an Ojibwa Community*. "Nobody explained what mercury is or how people get sick from it. All they told us was not to eat the fish any more. Next thing that happened was that Barney Lamm closed down Ball Lake Lodge, and suddenly, everybody who guided for Barney was out of a job."

The town of Grassy Narrows (known in the Ojibway language as "Asubpeeschoseewagong") had the misfortune of being 130 kilometres downstream from Dryden.

Only seven years earlier, in 1963, the town had been forcibly relocated by the government, causing local resentment and the breakdown of traditional order on the reserve.

The Whitedog reserve, 70 kilometres west of Grassy Narrows, was also affected. The two reserves had a population of 850 in 1970, and virtually all the inhabitants reported some form of mercury poisoning sickness.

Mercury is highly poisonous. It travels through a victim's blood and later reaches their heart, brain, kidneys and intestine. In the brain, it can damage the cerebellum, causing victims to experience blurred vision, shaking, mood swings and depression. It eventually leads to inability to walk or to remember simple things, and also causes feelings of numbness, physical deformity, deafness and partial blindness. Unborn fetuses can be killed. There is no cure or treatment.

The dangers of mercury poisoning in Ontario's waters were first identified in the late '60s at the University of Western Ontario. Norwegian undergraduate student Norvald Fimreite complained of feeling ill after eating fish from Lake St. Clair, and he went on to do a comprehensive study of poisonings in the lower Great Lakes. As a result, the Lake St. Clair's fisheries were permanently closed down.

Mercury poisoning has been known in Europe since at least the 16th century. In fact, the phrase "mad as a hatter" refers to the shaking and stumbling apparently common among hat makers. This was due to the mercury used in curing felt.

"Sometimes I can't sleep at night. My legs from the knees down feel numb.... I have a tingling sensation, like a thousand needles. My hands and tongue feel that way too. There's a tightness around my forehead, as if someone had tied twine around my head real tight. I take pills to sleep," said an unidentified Grassy Narrows resident to Shkilnyk.

> *The doctor tells me it's 'cause of what I was eating... the fish. But I don't know what it is. I worry about my family. I used to guide for twenty years in the summer. Every day I used to bring home fish. One day I got a letter from the government saying that I had a high mercury level. I think it was over 200. The letter said I was "at risk." But what does that mean? What does 200 mean for me, when everybody else is supposed to have 20? I sometimes get angry at this here mercury...but I don't know what to do about it.*

Symptoms of mercury poisoning are hard to identify, mainly because they resemble those of alcoholism, diabetes and Parkinson's disease. The poison can be identified in hair samples, but the extent of damage can only be found after the victim has died. A post-mortem of the brain reveals shrunken and damaged cells.

Because of these factors, the federal Ministry of Indian and Northern Affairs still insists that a direct link between the community's health problems and the poisoning cannot be proven.

With the economy of Grassy Narrows—based on fishing and guiding—eliminated overnight, over 90 percent of its inhabitants were on welfare by 1970. Shrewd lodge owners on the English and Wabigoon rivers neglected to mention to patrons that they might face permanent illness if they ate fish from the rivers. Instead, after a year, signs warning about poisoning were removed.

The Ontario government was initially hostile to compensation claims in the area.

A team of Japanese scientists travelled to the area in the late 1970s. They had studied victims of the infamous Minamata industrial mercury poisoning in Japan and found similar levels of poison in Grassy Narrows. Provincial Minister of Natural Resources Leo Bernier dismissed them on CBC television as "Japanese troubadours." He later apologized for the remark but remained unwilling to recognize the scope of the problem.

CBC reporter Warner Troyer recorded a conversation between the vice president of Reed Paper Ltd., which owned Dryden Chemicals, and Environment Minister George Kerr. "George, we made $80,000 profit last year—I can't tell my directors that we have to spend to $15 million to clean up pollution," said the vice president. Bernier later chimed in on the vice president's side, saying "That's right George. He can't do that. You can see that..."

It was not until 1985 that the federal and provincial governments offered compensation to the victims of the poisoning. The people of the Grassy Narrows and Whitedog First Nations received $16.7 million, with $5.75 million coming from Reed Paper and $6 million from another guilty pulp mill, Great Lakes Forest Products Ltd.

"Whatever money we get from the settlement will never be enough to replace what we lost," Chief Arnold Pelly told CBC. In fact, Grassy Narrows continues to argue that they haven't received all of the promised settlement. In 2000, talks between the community and the federal government broke down.

The economy of the area remains devastated, and many older residents who ate fish during the period are now crippled with physical and mental injuries. Living off the land, the traditional habit of the remote town's inhabitants, is no longer possible. Imported fish offered to

Grassy Narrows' residents by the federal government was reported as being mushy and tasteless.

It will take over 50 years—some have estimated as high as 100—for the mercury levels to go down to a safe limit.

The mercury disaster has received international attention, particularly in the United States and Japan. Japanese photographer Hiro Miyamatsu lived in Grassy Narrows for years, documenting the social and economic collapse of the community. In 2002, Japanese researcher Dr. Masazumi Harada returned to Grassy Narrows to conduct another study. Of the 60 people studied in Grassy Narrows and Whitedog, 70 percent showed symptoms of mercury poisoning. The eight people originally tested in 1975 all showed symptoms worsening.

A play performed at the Whitedog Reserve in 1980 by the Theatre Max company, called "Whitedog/Cat's Dance," told the story of the disaster. Subsequent media coverage has made Grassy Narrows and Whitedog well known across the province.

Today at Grassy Narrows, the tragedy of mercury poisoning is compounded with a momentous struggle around historic treaty rights. The community is now involved in a bitter struggle against the logging companies Weyerhauser and Abitibi, which are cutting forests that residents consider part of their traditional hunting territory. For the past few years, Grassy Narrows residents have set up blockades along logging roads.

Air Canada Flight 621 Crash

ONTARIO'S MOST DEADLY AIR DISASTER took place on July 6, 1970, when an error in communication caused an Air Canada flight to crash, killing everyone on board. The Douglas DC-8 was on route from Montréal to Los Angeles but was stopping for a layover in Toronto.

The plane's captain and its first officer had a long-standing disagreement on when to lift the spoilers to slow the aircraft down during landing. The captain apparently preferred to lift them just after the plane had hit the ground, whereas the first officer preferred to do this just before the plane landed. They made a compromise that either man could do it his way when the other man was leading the landing.

For reasons that are unknown—most likely just sloppiness—the opposite happened on July 5. That is, the captain told the first officer to do the opposite of their usual routine. The first officer, perhaps not listening closely to the instructions, instead followed the usual pattern of lifting the spoilers just before the landing, without giving an explanation. As a result of the poor coordination, the plane slowed down too soon and hit the runway at a poor angle with great force.

The plane's fourth engine broke off from the force of the impact, leaving a trail of flaming fuel behind it. The captain took off again, with the idea of making another landing attempt. However, he was told by the control tower operators that there was now an unsafe amount of debris on the ground and that they should move to another runway.

As the aircraft was circling around in the air, a few minutes after the initial botched landing, its right wing caught on fire. Apparently the loss of the engine had torn off part of the wing, causing it to leak highly flammable fuel. The fire from the fuel tank quickly spread to the remaining third engine on the right side, causing it to explode and break off. By that point, the entire right wing of the plane had been blown off, and the aircraft went into a sudden high-speed nose-dive. At 8:10 PM—five minutes before its scheduled arrival—the DC-8 crashed head-on into a field in Brampton, near the airport. All 100 passengers and nine crew members were instantly killed.

Many of the passengers on board had been Americans, returning from a July 4 long weekend of sightseeing in Montréal. A number of others were off-duty Air Canada employees, taking advantage of discount flights the airline had offered them.

The plane landed only 90 metres from the home where trucker Sytze Burgma lived with his wife and seven children. The plane's wing came to rest only 12 metres from his back door. (Unique among airports, Toronto Pearson International Airport is closely surrounded by houses and apartments. The safety of this situation has often been criticized as a disaster waiting to happen.)

Sytze, a Dutch immigrant who had survived the Blitzkreig of World War II, said, "There were bits of stuff sprinkling down like yellow snow—I guess it was insulation. I listened for screams or anything, but there was just a hissing sound. There was nobody left to help.... In the old country I saw planes come down pretty close to my house but they had been shot down. I've lived here for four years and watched planes come and go and never fearing a thing—then this happens."

John Burgma, son of Sytze, told the *Globe and Mail*, "I'd just listened to the 8 o'clock news on the radio when I heard a hissing and crackling in the sky. It was getting louder so I looked out the back window and saw this plane coming down at me... One side was covered with flames and I couldn't see the right wing for fire. Then it hit with an awful roar... I was scared. I figured we were goners. I went out but I saw nothing at all. They (the passengers) didn't have a chance."

Sytze's neighbours, the Day family, also believed the plane was heading directly for their house. Mrs. Day and her daughter watched the aircraft hit the ground 450 metres from their house. "A big part fell off—it looked like a wing—and I grabbed Barbara and ran out of the house into the field, but I couldn't tell which way to run to get out of the way," Day told *The Globe*. "Other little pieces seemed to be falling off. I think it flew almost over the house. Then it crashed."

The impact of the crash left a hole in the earth 2 metres deep and 11 metres in diameter. The decapitated body of a child was found thrown from the wreckage, with clenched fists. Part of a flight attendant's uniform was seen hanging from a nearby elm tree, burnt by the fire.

To this day, remains of the airplane and bone fragments from its passengers are still being dug up in the field. A group of relatives of the deceased passengers and crew continues to demand that the government perform a complete excavation of the field to remove the rest of the human remains for burial.

The crash of flight 621 remains the worst aviation disaster in Ontario history, and the second worst in Canada, after a 1963 crash in Ste-Thérèse, Québec, in which 118 people were killed.

Barrie Highway Collision

HIGHWAY 400, BETWEEN BARRIE AND TORONTO, is frequently crammed with long-distance commuters and cottage goers. It forms the beginning of the route between Toronto and northern Ontario and onwards to western Canada. As well as the movement of people, the massive provincial highway forms the route of many transport trucks, bringing goods north and raw materials south.

Accidents are not uncommon on the 400, but nothing has been seen—before or since—that compares with the disaster on Sunday, March 18, 1973.

Some 12 kilometres south of Barrie, a minor collision occurred in the southbound side of the highway. While police and tow truck drivers went about their work, other drivers waited to pass the area. A number of tightly packed cars began to build up, looking for the first opportunity to get past the bottleneck. A late snowstorm had covered the highway with ice and slush and was making vision difficult. OPP officer Ed Kelso later estimated that visibility was probably no more than between 7 and 10 metres.

The sudden slowdown in traffic and hostile weather conditions seem to have been lost on the driver of a lumber truck. At 5:30 PM, the huge vehicle, dragging a pup trailer behind it, was speeding south on the highway. Unable to reduce its speed, the truck smashed directly into the back of the rows of stopped cars. The truck then flipped over, crushing a number of cars under its weight and blocking much of the road. Its cargo of logs, weighing over 40 tonnes, spilled out across the road.

Only seconds later, a bus belonging to Ontario Northland (the provincially owned transit service) came upon the scene. It swerved to avoid the jack-knifed truck, only to crash into more of the stopped cars itself.

What began as a minor fender-bender had turned into a flaming 31-vehicle pileup. Many drivers and passengers were trapped in crushed cars. Those who did not die instantly were unable to escape the roaring fire that developed as engines, gasoline and logs caught fire. One car was flattened to 25 centimetres.

A driver who survived the collision later told reporters that his car had—within a span of seconds—been hit by four different vehicles. His car gradually crumpled around him. He had been pushed into the stopped cars by the force of the lumber truck. Looking out the window, he saw "fire which flowed toward my car almost like a river." It was only with luck that he and the passengers in his car—his wife and mother—were able to crawl out through a rear window and make it to safety before the fire engulfed their vehicle.

The fire was not contained until 11 o'clock that night. It took rescue crews a day to remove all the bodies and to clear the highway of wreckage. The heat of the blaze was so extreme that patches of asphalt on the road caught fire and melted. Before the highway could be reopened, work crews had to repatch the whole stretch of road.

Many of the victims had been burned beyond recognition and had to be identified by vehicle ownership and dental records. "We're going by blobs rather than people," one shocked police constable told the *Globe and Mail*. Most of the police on the scene said they had never before seen such a horrific crash. Blowtorches and hacksaws had to be used to extract survivors and bodies from the wreckage. In some cases, shovels were used to remove human remains.

Some licence plates had even been melted. These vehicles had to be identified through serial numbers on their parts.

"People on our bus began to panic," said Susan Hughes of Barrie in *The Globe*. She was travelling in a northbound bus on the other side of the highway. As the bus approached the area, flames could be seen from as far away as 3.5 kilometres. "Some of [the bus passengers] started to cry and wail when they saw it...we had seen so many accidents on the way up." As they passed the scene, Hughes described one car as being "literally covered with blood."

A total of 12 people died, mostly as a result of burns. Another 43 suffered injuries.

In the aftermath of the pileup, most of the blame fell onto the driver of the log truck. Amazingly, he escaped from the accident uninjured; the driver of the Ontario Northland bus, by contrast, had both of his legs broken by the impact. It was considered that the truck was driving much too quickly and recklessly, given the snowstorm conditions.

The truck was also on the road illegally. At the time, the provincial Lord's Day Act was still in place. This not only kept shops from being open on Sundays but also prohibited trucks from being on the road without special permission. The safety of the pup trailer being pulled by the truck was also questioned.

In the provincial inquest that followed the accident, truck mechanic R.W. Stapley inspected the truck and testified that it had been extremely poorly maintained. Before the accident, it had broken springs, the tread of several tires had been worn off as well as—amazingly—two flat tires and defective brakes. Stapley reported that all the brakes on the trailer were also defective.

"It would have been impossible to stop that truck in any form of emergency," he told the inquest. "There were no brakes on the trailer. The brake defects would cause a tendency to swerve. If the brakes were applied, the tractor would want to stop, but the trailer would want to go on. That's one quick way to cause a jack-knife."

Snow buildup on the road was higher than it normally was at that time of year. Not expecting such a late snowstorm, the Ministry of Transport had removed the snow fences protecting the highway only nine days earlier.

Bus-Train Crash

TORONTO TRANSIT COMMISSION DRIVER DONALD SINE faced the ultimate fear of many drivers when his bus stalled while crossing a set of railway tracks. Sine was no newcomer to the job. He had been driving buses for 21 years and had received a safety award just the previous year.

The time was 4:45 PM on December 12, 1975. Sine was taking his usual route, through the Toronto suburb of Scarborough, heading towards Warden subway station. It was rush hour and the bus was nearly at full capacity, with 50 passengers on board.

At a previous stop, two passengers had forced the back door of the bus open, in order to get off. The doors did not close properly and were jerked open as the bus crossed the tracks. Because the bus was designed to automatically prevent movement while the doors were open, its engine was disabled. Less than five seconds after the bus had stalled, the bell rang to indicate that a train was coming, and the guard rails came down on top of the vehicle.

Sine was unable to restart the bus' engine. The tracks, near St. Clair Ave. E., were immediately beside Scarborough Station, and Sine knew that a commuter GO train would be coming along the track any minute. He moved to get the passengers off his bus and to safety.

Nearly all of the passengers had been removed from the bus when the train hit; however, five or six were stuck behind. Everyone seemed stunned by the situation and did not immediately realize the danger they were in.

Matters quickly came to a horrible climax. The GO train sped towards the bus at over 110 kilometres per hour. Its engineer noticed the bus, but by this point there was no time to stop. He slammed on the emergency brakes, but this only slowed the train slightly.

The train hit the bus, spinning it around and throwing it off the tracks and against the railway crossing sign. The force was so great that many were killed instantly. Surprisingly, the majority of the victims were actually among those who had left the bus. A number of them were standing too close to the bus and were hit by parts of the vehicle as it flew through the air. One woman who was hit by the bus was thrown 6 metres through the air, hitting the ground face-first. She was found unconscious, but alive.

One body, however, was found half a kilometre down the tracks. Others were trapped under a fence next to the tracks.

"The driver yelled out that a train was coming and asked everyone to get off..." 13-year-old David Reive told the *Globe and Mail*. "Everyone was running to get off. No one was really panicking. They were just getting off the bus the way we do at the subway station when it's rush hour. I got off and started running and got hit by a piece of the bus."

"I saw the train coming," said Alice Mooney. "[I] got off safely, then realized the bus was still on the tracks, and I thought, 'He's not going to stop.' Then I thought, 'He's going to miss the bus, thank God.' Then, Wham."

Mrs. Rate, who lived nearby and witnessed the accident, called it "just one ungodly crash. We heard the bells going—meaning the [level crossing] gates and signals were working. We heard the diesel's horn blaring and then that ungodly crash."

Nine passengers died in the incident and 21 were injured. Ambulances on the scene found it difficult to deal with so many injured at one time. The bus driver, Sine, was taken to hospital and treated for shock but was not injured. No one aboard the train was injured. Scratch marks on the engine were the only sign that the crash had occurred.

Later investigation showed that little could have been done differently to prevent the crash. An ambulance-bus was developed for use in Toronto shortly afterwards, in order to treat large numbers of victims quickly. The railway crossing was later replaced by an underpass, to allow traffic to flow faster and to prevent future disasters.

Air Canada Flight 189 Crash

June 26, 1978
Toronto

A DISASTROUS AIR CRASH occurred on June 26, 1978, when an airplane failed to take off properly from Toronto Pearson International Airport. The Air Canada flight was travelling from Ottawa to Vancouver, making stops in Toronto and Winnipeg.

At 8:15 AM, the plane was taking off from Toronto when one of its tires popped and debris became lodged in the wheel. The aircraft's automatic warning system informed the pilot, Reginald W. Stewart, that it was unsafe to continue with the takeoff, so Stewart tried to bring the aircraft to a stop, but only after delaying for four crucial seconds. By this point, the plane was already racing at a speed of almost 300 kilometres per hour and was two-thirds of the way down the runway. Before it could be stopped or turned around, the plane had overshot the end of the runway and smashed down into the Etobicoke Creek bed, an 18-metre drop.

"I heard the backfiring and banging noises as it was coming down the runway," 16-year-old Mark Yepalaar, who was working close to the crash site, told the *Globe and Mail*. "That's what got me. I'm used to the sound of airplanes, being so close to the airport and all, that this was unusual. I ran to the window and saw the plane go right over the embankment and into the ravine."

Dorothy Morgan, of Nanaimo, was on board the plane and later described the experience as "a rolling, like someone dragging a lead ball along the road and it was bumpy.

Then it felt like the captain was trying to put on the brakes because it didn't feel like a natural takeoff at all. I felt good until I saw the trees... Then I realized we were going over the cliff and I started to shout 'Lord have mercy, Lord have mercy.'"

The passengers remained calm at first, but began to panic when they discovered that one of the emergency doors was jammed. Some passengers were forced to escape through the holes in the plane's fuselage that was punctured during the crash.

Clarence Nolan, a supervisor for the Metro Toronto Ambulance Service, praised the operation. "It was the most organized and calm disaster that I have ever attended in 20 years. It is the finest evacuation I have ever seen. I have been at plane crashes, I have been at boat disasters, I have been at multiple-alarm fires. I have never seen anything go as well as this."

Luckily, a fire did not break out—which would likely have been fatal for the 102 passengers and 5 crew members on board—and doctors were on the scene within 15 minutes. However, the plane broke into three pieces, and the force of the impact injured many of those on the plane.

Two passengers were killed. Toronto passenger Irwin Theodore Child, 45, was crushed to death when the seat in front of his came off its moorings. Another passenger, J. Frank Scrase, 78, of Victoria, was killed when one of his ribs became dislodged and punctured his heart. All 105 survivors reported injuries.

Musician Bobby Gimby (who had composed "CA-NA-DA," the Expo '67 theme) was on the flight and survived the crash. "I sitting right up front and saw it all," he said. "I just held on tight. I guess I was one of the lucky ones."

An inquiry into the crash blamed the accident on a number of factors, starting with the pilot's delay in response to the warning. It also criticized the design of the airport—which had a number of natural features such as ravines, rivers and forests near the edges of its runways. In addition, the plane's wing had narrowly missed hitting navigational lights at the end of the runway, which likely would have set off explosions in the plane's fuel tanks. It also came close to hitting an above-ground power line that controlled all the navigational lights.

Mississauga Train Derailment

ON NOVEMBER 10, 1979, a CPR freight train pulling 106 cars derailed in the Toronto suburb of Mississauga. The train was loaded with many toxic chemicals, including liquid chlorine, propane, styrene and toluene. The result was the biggest evacuation North America had ever seen, and the biggest it was to see, until Hurricane Katrina necessitated the evacuation of New Orleans in 2005.

The train, known as CP #106, was coming from Windsor and arrived in Mississauga around midnight. Some of the wheels on the train were not properly lubricated, and a dangerous amount of friction was being produced. The wheel bearing in the 33rd car began to heat up, and the axle melted through it as a result. Witnesses reported seeing sparks flying out from underneath the car as it was dragged along over the tracks near Burnhamthorpe Road.

At 11:53 PM, the derailment began, with one car after another being dragged off the tracks by the weight of the damaged boxcar. A total of 21 boxcars crashed, falling off the tracks and in some cases splitting open. Eleven of these cars carried propane, four had caustic soda, three with styrene, two with fibreglass insulation and one had chlorine—an extremely dangerous mix. Many of the chemicals spilled out over the tracks and nearby roadways near the intersection of Mavis Road and Dundas Street.

The massive explosion awoke the entire city from its slumber. Flames reached 1.5 kilometres into the air.

Fire crews who were called to the scene immediately grasped the seriousness of the situation. "When I arrived just before midnight, I thought many of us would not live through the night," firefighter Cyril Hare later told the *Toronto Star*.

Railway worker Larry Krupa braved the fire and chemicals to separate the still-secure 32nd car from the derailed 33rd. Because of his efforts, the engineers were able to move the front of the train away from the derailment and prevent the 32 cars—many of which also contained chemicals—from catching fire.

Before police arrived to push them back, a crowd formed around the derailed cars. A second explosion occurred, throwing them to the ground and shooting pieces of twisted metal in all directions. Luckily, no one was killed.

The reverberations of the second explosion were so strong that it shattered windows up to one kilometre away. Three greenhouses and a municipal recreation centre were destroyed, and a green, chemical haze was seen in the air. A propane tank from the train was fired through the air a distance of 700 metres.

A third explosion then went off, as another propane car caught fire. The force of this explosion launched the entire car 65 metres.

But what firefighters feared most was that the chlorine tank could catch fire. Chlorine was by far the most toxic chemical on the train, and it had the potential to suffocate hundreds of thousands of people if released into the air. Being heavier than air, chlorine gas spreads over the ground rather than dispersing upwards when it is released. The car containing the chlorine was punctured.

Fire crews fight flames when a 106-car freight train derailed in Mississauga in 1979. Explosions and fears of a liquid chlorine spill prompted a mass evacuation.

Within two hours of the crash, 3500 residents in the area were evacuated, as well as 1400 patients in a hospital close to the crash site. By morning, 218,000 people had been evacuated—almost all of Mississauga's 284,000 residents—along with three hospitals and six nursing homes. Emergency crews had determined that if the chlorine escaped, an area of the city as wide as 25 square kilometres would be affected.

Mississauga had become a ghost town overnight.

Many evacuees went to stay with family or friends. Those who had nobody else to turn to were housed in an emergency centre set up in the Square One Mall, 3 kilometres northeast of the crash. Although suffering a sprained ankle, newly elected Mississauga mayor Hazel McCallion quickly arrived on the scene to personally oversee the relief efforts (McCallion, Canada's longest serving mayor, still remains in office today).

To prevent further explosions, emergency crews kept the derailed cars cool, and the fire was allowed to burn itself out. One of the propane cars continued to burn for two days. The chlorine car, which was slowly leaking, never released all its contents. Its puncture was patched, and the tank was safely emptied on November 19.

No life-threatening injuries occurred as a result of the derailment. A news camera operator broke his leg because of the force of one of the explosions, and eight firefighters were treated for small amounts of chlorine inhalation.

Residents, however, were not allowed to return to the area for six days. The Queen Elizabeth Way, one of Canada's busiest highways, remained closed for a week because it passed through the evacuated area.

Many cities were impressed with the speed and efficiency of Mississauga's evacuation, and the procedures it used became standardized across the continent. A number of improvements were made in laws surrounding freight train safety, including mandatory detectors on each car that would indicate if their wheels were beginning to overheat and a lower maximum speed when passing through residential areas. Also added were rules governing what kind of chemicals could be transported together and what the order and proximity of the cars could be.

Nursing Home Fire

ON JULY 14, 1980, a fire began at 9:30 PM on the top floor of the Extendacare Nursing Home. Located across the street from Mississauga's General Hospital, the residence was home to many seniors who were hospital outpatients, suffering from serious illnesses or injuries. In total, 198 people lived in the three-storey building, which was equipped with 202 beds.

Those with the worst conditions and the most frail physical states were housed on the top floor.

Alice Sinden, a resident on the top floor, was the first to notice the smoke. She called her grandson in Etobicoke, who in turn called the fire department. Witnesses to the fire described it as looking like the flame from a giant blowtorch shooting down the corridor.

Christine Gage, a nursing assistant working on the first floor, learned about the fire from frantic patients. "I went up to the third floor with a fire extinguisher and tried to put out the fire," she told the *Globe and Mail*. "But the smoke was too thick and I couldn't fight it, so we started to rush the residents out."

However, she was forced to close the doors to the third floor, leaving its residents behind, in order to save those on the lower floors. Although the fire doors were not locked, most of the third-floor residents were too frail to walk, let alone run through the smoke and push the doors open.

Firefighters managed to put the fire out within an hour, and emergency crews from across the street rushed patients into the General Hospital. Tremendous amounts of smoke remained in the building, and what should have been an easy rescue—given the nursing home's location next to the hospital—turned into a deadly disaster.

Some residents were rescued by firefighters using ropes and ladders. In the end, 21 residents died, mostly from smoke inhalation. Another 35 were injured in the fire.

Betty Tyres, a private nurse who lived nearby, came running to the building to help the survivors. "The confused ones were smiling," she told *The Globe*. "They didn't know what it was all about. Some of them were crying." Tyres and other volunteers from the neighbourhood were credited with saving a number of lives.

The exact cause of the fire was never determined. It was guessed that although smoking was strictly forbidden in the building, one of the seniors on the top floor might have sneaked a cigarette. The butt might have started the fire. A few witnesses reported hearing explosions on the third floor, probably caused by the fire as it reached the nursing home's oxygen tanks, which were stored there.

Luckily, such a fire would be unlikely to occur today. In 1980, building codes in Mississauga did not mandate sprinkler systems to be installed on every floor. As a result, only the basement of the Extendacare Nursing Home was set up with sprinklers. The fire prompted stricter safety regulations to be put in place.

Air Ontario Flight 1363 Crash

AIR ONTARIO FLIGHT 1363 CRASHED a mere 15 seconds after taking off from Dryden airport on a snowy March day.

The small 16-year-old plane had stopped off in the town on its way between Thunder Bay and Winnipeg. However, the aircraft had not been properly deiced before takeoff. It was also overloaded with baggage, dangerously over the maximum weight allowed for its size. As a result, it was simply too heavy to achieve any kind of height and crashed head-on into the forest, 1.5 kilometres from the end of the runway.

Although rescue crews arrived quickly, the intensity of the fire caused by the crash made rescuing passengers difficult. It quickly spread into the forest, burning an area 30 metres wide and half a kilometre long. Heavy snows also made it difficult to get ambulances and fire trucks near the site. Local residents rushed out to help, bringing snowploughs and chainsaws to help clear away snow buildup and trees in the area.

"We heard the plane pass over our house then we heard a loud thump," George Groves told the *Globe and Mail*. He lived only half a kilometre from the runway. Gordon Tomlinson, who lived nearby, also heard a loud noise and immediately saw smoke coming from the airport.

Firefighters noted that only the nose and tail of the plane looked intact. "It's a total mess and the entire fuselage is broken up in pieces. Debris is scattered all over the place and just the tail appears intact," reported one fire-fighter. The fire and explosions had blown off the roof of the plane. The entire middle portion of the aircraft was pulverized and burned. After landing in the forest, it rolled 275 metres down a hill and broke into three sections. The largest remaining fragment was a 6-metre piece of the wing, thrown some distance from the plane.

The horrendous collision caused the deaths of 21 of the 65 passengers on board and 3 of the 4 crew members. A total of 22 people burned to death during the crash, while two others later died of their injuries in hospital. Survivors were treated for burns, fractured bones and shock. Some of the most seriously hurt had to be airlifted to Winnipeg for operations.

As survivor Danny Godin later told the *Globe and Mail*, "Most of the people in the very front of the plane did not get out.... The plane quivered as if we had an air disturbance...(and it) exploded into flames when it first hit the tree tops."

Another survivor, Bryon Adams, said, "I was pinned there, my foot was jammed under the seats ahead of me with the flames about 20 feet away. There were people running over me, falling over me.... Everyone was panicking. I remember this woman yelling: 'My baby. My baby.'" A member of Adams' curling team, also on the plane, rescued him by getting his foot unstuck.

Richard Campbell of Saskatoon found his clothes on fire. "I know I went over at least six charred bodies," he said. "I went out through the cockpit. Other people were falling out right into the snow."

Another passengers saw "gallons of fuel rush past us. Seconds later, it was all in flames."

Mrs. Ditmars, who survived the crash, credited the pilot with keeping the plane's nose up when it hit the trees.

"The big thing was to get away, because we were waiting for the explosion," she said. "We got about 100 feet away, and it (the plane) just burst into flames. Anybody that was there was gone. I was just so happy to be alive."

The plane's black box, which would have provided invaluable information into the cause of the crash, was itself burnt beyond recognition. Since black boxes are made out of special material and were previously considered indestructible, the intense heat and violence of the crash can be attested to.

An inquiry into the crash blamed the plane's pilot, and Air Ontario management, for trying to cut corners to save money. The pilot had apparently not asked ground crews to deice the plane's wings, despite the obviously icy conditions, and had pushed to leave the airport as soon as possible regardless of the danger.

"Pilots know generally about the dangers of ice, but I don't think they understand how little ice it takes to have disastrous consequences," Peter Boag of the Canadian Aviation Safety Board said. A feud between the Board and the Federal Ministry of Transport may have slowed the passing of information on deicing safety.

As a result of the crash, a number of changes were made to federal air safety regulations, strictly preventing planes from taking off with any ice on their wings and specifying the exact steps for deicing.

Hagersville Tire Fire

February 1990
Hagersville (Haldimand County)

ONE OF SOUTHERN ONTARIO'S WORST fire disasters of recent times began in the early morning hours of February 12, 1990. Youths who had broken into the Tyre King dump outside of Hagersville began burning old tires there.

The fire quickly spread across the two-hectare dump, eventually burning between 12 and 14 million tires. It took firefighters, under the coordination of the Ministry of Natural Resources, 17 days to contain the blaze, even with the assistance of three CL-215 water bombers. The planes worked in continuous cycles, picking up water from nearby Lake Erie and dropping it over the flames. Over 40 firefighters worked on the ground, trying to isolate heaps of burning tires and to put them out with water and foam. One firefighter even took the time to save a raccoon trapped on the roof of one of the burning buildings near the dump.

Tires are notorious for being easily combustible—and they contain toxic chemicals such as carbon monoxide and sulphur dioxide that can be released when burned. Tires burn hotter than wood, and their shape produces more draft. Firefighters are said to especially hate fighting a fire of burning tires because of the danger posed by their wire beading, which can trip and injure rescuers, and the carcinogenic smoke they give off.

The toxic smoke from the fire forced the evacuation of all residents within a 5-kilometre radius around the dump, including all 2500 citizens of Hagersville. Residents were not allowed to return to their homes for 16 days.

Witnesses reported that the smoke rose over one kilometre into the sky and could be seen almost 100 kilometres away.

The oil produced from the melting tires also seeped into the ground, causing long-lasting environmental damage in a rural area where many people relied on wells for their water and farming for their livelihood. Over the following year, 225,000 litres of oil were pumped out of the site. However, as late as 1998, there were local reports of oil seeping out of the soil on rainy days. The site of the fire remains closed off.

After the fire had been put out, much of the blame was placed on Tyre King dump owner Edward Straza. He had earlier been ordered by the Ministry of the Environment to take more fire preventative measures and to build a reservoir on his property. Straza had refused to comply and was delaying the process by filing a series of appeals at the time of the fire. Straza's punishment, however, wasn't delayed—his house, located near the dump, was burned to the ground by the fire. Five local teenagers were later charged and convicted for their part in starting the fire. Luckily, no deaths or injuries were caused by the blaze.

Blame for the disaster probably also rests with the insatiable hunger for tires that Ontarians seem to have. With the province's massive auto industry and demand for vehicles, some 12 million scrap tires are produced in Ontario each year. Less than half that number are recycled annually, so most of them continue to end up in places like the Tyre King dump. To reduce the scale of possible fires, provincial laws don't allow more than 5000 tires to be stored in one place—but many illegal dumps exist, tucked away in remote parts of the countryside, or in some cases the tires are piled up in old warehouses.

Cobalt Highway Crash

July 30, 1991
Cobalt (Timiskaming District)

ONE OF CANADA'S WORST highway crashes took place on July 30, 1991. At 3 am, in the darkness of a northern Ontario night, a packed Dodge minivan was travelling on Highway 11 (sometimes known as Yonge St.). Road conditions were poor, with heavy rains rendering the pavement slippery, and—even with high beams on—it was difficult for drivers to see far ahead.

The group of 11 passengers in the minivan included four children. As well as several Calgarians, there were also visitors from Jamaica and Britain. The group had started in Calgary and were on route to Ottawa for a family reunion. For some reason, they had opted to take Highway 11 across the remote north, rather than the more popular Trans-Canada Highway.

Just north of the town of Cobalt, the minivan crossed the yellow line on the road and found itself in the wrong lane, going the wrong direction. The weather conditions, combined with a bend ahead in the road, obscured an oncoming truck from the minivan's driver. A head-on collision occurred, destroying the minivan and killing all the people on board.

The truck driver, Real Laroque, age 54, was unhurt. "I would have taken the ditch to avoid them, knowing I would have gotten killed myself," he told the *Globe and Mail*. "There was nothing I could do. They slammed head-on into me."

The curve on that stretch of Highway 11 had developed a notorious reputation, having been the scene of several previous crashes. It was also speculated—given the late hour—that the driver of the minivan might have drifted off while navigating the quiet northern road.

Toronto Subway Crash

＊＊＊

August 11, 1995
Toronto

THE SCENARIO OF A SUBWAY CRASH is painful to envision. The feelings of claustrophobia, the entrapment in a dark tunnel, the image of smoke filling the air, and the inability to escape, are all the stuff of nightmares. Fortunately, subway crashes are very rare. The tightly controlled environment of underground rapid transit prevents the sort of accidents that often occur on highways or railways. However, one serious subway disaster did occur in Toronto on August 11, 1995.

Between St. Clair West and Dupont stations, a southbound train went through two red lights at a speed of 56 kilometres per hour. The track between the two stations slopes down sharply as the line passes under Spadina Hill, causing trains to pick up speed. Unfortunately, the train's brakes and emergency brakes both failed, and its inexperienced driver was unable to slow the train. Robert Jeffrey —working his second day on the job—misunderstood the red lights, thinking that they were only warnings.

An automatic "trip arm" should have activated the train's brakes as it passed the red lights, but it also failed. Worn-down wheels and rails had shifted the train into a slightly different position, out of the reach of the trip arm.

At 6:02 PM, the train speeding downhill collided with a stationary train on the same track. Passengers at the opposite ends of both trains experienced little more than a jolt and some loud noise—but the effect was devastating. The front car was forced underneath the back of the last car in the stationary train, causing the two to overlap each other by more than 5 metres. Police Sergeant Nigel Fontaine, one of the first rescuers to arrive, described the effect as looking "like an accordion."

Some 150 firefighters, 100 paramedics and 130 police officers were soon on the scene. Emergency workers trying to rescue the 700 passengers were shocked by the extent of the damage. The tunnel quickly filled with dust and black smoke. The crash cut off power in the tunnel, causing ventilation systems to fail. The temperature soon reached over 40°C. Air Canada staff was brought in to hook up a huge air conditioning system designed especially for aircraft.

One subway passenger, Girgis Sadd, later recalled that after the crash, the subway remained eerily quiet for three minutes. Then, a sound "like a bomb" went off, and the force shook most passengers to the ground. Twisted metal and debris was thrown in all directions, and there was fear that a serious fire could break out.

One nurse working on the rescue said that the victims "looked like they were coming from a coal mine. Their hair, their clothes, their faces were all covered with soot."

Rescuers had difficulty working in the stifling heat and surrounding dust. A team of surgeons had to be brought down to amputate a woman's leg, which had become trapped under debris. Kinga Szabo's leg was removed, but the woman later died of her injuries in hospital. In all, three passengers—Szabo, Christina Munar Reyes and Xian Hui Lin—died in the crash. Over a hundred others were injured, some very seriously.

The train's driver was among those severely injured, and he never returned to the job.

The Spadina line of Toronto's subway system was closed for five days following the disaster while a cleanup and investigation took place. The accident was blamed on poor maintenance and insufficient training of staff.

The Toronto Transit Commission (TTC) improved its driver training program and began disciplining drivers who ran red lights to save time. The TTC also redesigned the trip arms and replaced worn-down trains and wheels across much of the subway system.

Walkerton *E. Coli* Poisoning

DESPITE THE MANY APPEALING FEATURES of the town of Walkerton, its name is now permanently fixed in many people's minds as a synonym for disaster. The town's name was put onto the national and international map by a series of events in May 2000 that became known as the Walkerton Tragedy.

On May 15, many of Walkerton's 5000 residents began to experience health problems, such as nausea, dehydration, bloody diarrhea and kidney failure. Retrospectively, the symptoms were identified as the classic signs of the deadly O157:H7 strain of *E. coli* bacteria.

(Although its name is usually abbreviated to "*E. coli*," the bacteria's full name is *Escherichia Coli*, after Dr. Theodore Escherich, the German scientist who discovered it in 1885. Most forms of *E. coli* are harmless—in fact, it is one of the most common bacteria in the human body. However, the strain *E. coli* O157:H7, first isolated in 1975, is highly toxic.)

E. coli outbreaks began occurring in North America during the 1980s and have mostly been blamed on large-scale industrial agriculture and poor drainage systems. Major cattle farms switched their cows from a diet of grasses to one of grains, which is more nutrient-rich and allows the animals to grow faster. However, a side effect seems to have been a change in the acidity of cows' stomachs, which encourages the bacteria to develop.

(Indeed, most *E. coli* infection cases come from eating undercooked hamburger meat.)

In addition, manure from cattle barns is sometimes not appropriately drained and stored appropriately and—as occurred in Walkerton—leaches into the water supply.

Between 2 and 7 percent of *E. coli* cases lead to fatal kidney failure—usually in the very young and very old.

Local officials in Walkerton were quick to downplay the possibility of *E. coli* poisoning after residents got sick. Indeed, it was not until May 21 that the town actually advised its citizens to stop drinking the local tap water without boiling it first. That was the same day the first death occurred.

However, by that point it was already considerably too late to save some of the town's most susceptible residents. Seven people died directly from *E. coli* poisoning, 14 seniors died from complications probably caused by the bacteria and 2300 people—more than half of Walkerton—became sick.

On May 25, in an interview with CBC Radio, Dr. Murray McQuigge was the first to suggest that the Walkerton Public Utilities Commission must have known about the problem before May 21.

Criticism was immediately focused on two brothers, Stan and Frank Koebel, who managed the town's water system. Neither had ever received any formal training in chemistry or engineering or in managing a water utility. During the week of the poisonings, both men vehemently claimed the water was safe to drink and denied that it could be contaminated with *E. coli*.

Walkerton's last provincial water inspection had been in February 1998. Traces of *E. coli* were discovered then, and improvements were recommended, but no follow-up was done. The town of Walkerton was concerned at the time and wrote to the province, asking that it resume regular testing. Private tests in January and April of 2000 revealed more *E. coli*, and the lab that found the results attempted five times to get the Ministry of the Environment to act on the findings. Eventually, the Ministry contacted the Walkerton Public Utilities Commission but did not notify the public health officer, something they were required to do.

More tests were conducted with a new lab, and dangerous levels of *E. coli* were discovered on May 16. The lab, A & L Canada Laboratories East Ltd., only sent the results to Stan Koebel of the Walkerton Public Utilities Commission, and it ordered him not to pass on the information to the provincial government. The lab claimed that the results of the test were intellectual property and that Walkerton would be forced to pay royalties if the tests were revealed to anyone.

Criminal charges were later pursued against the Koebels, and both made plea bargains in order to be charged with "public nuisance." As part of the bargain, the men admitted to falsifying safety reports over a long period of time, and Frank admitted to frequently being drunk on the job. On December 21, 2004, Stan was sentenced to one year in jail, and Frank was sentenced to nine months of house arrest. Stan continued to downplay his role in the tragedy, noting that he himself had contracted *E. coli* poisoning—though he recovered.

In his ruling, which took two hours to read out, Judge Bruce Durno said, "No sentence I could impose can assuage the enormous losses. But, the offenders are not being sentenced for being the cause of the Walkerton water tragedy." Durno determined that Stan Koebel knew that the water was contaminated as early as May 17 but waited four days before admitting it to the public, in the hopes that the problem would simply go away.

The total cost associated with the poisoning was estimated at $64.5 million. If personal suffering of victims and their families were added into the picture, that figure would increase to $155 million. The cost to Walkerton's businesses—for things like purchasing bottled water and disinfecting pipes—was pegged at $651,422, and lost revenue was estimated at $2.7 million. It cost $9 million to fix the town's water system. The government spent $3.5 million on legal fees and another $1.5 million to supply clean water to public institutions in the area during the crisis.

Initially, most citizens of Walkerton strongly criticized the Koebels for their negligence, but later public opinion seemed to soften towards them. Many contended that blame rested on the provincial government, which was in charge of water safety across the province.

Under Premier Mike Harris, funding for public utilities and the Ministry of the Environment had been cut back. A total of 42 percent of the Ministry's budget was eliminated, along with 900 of its 2400 front-line staff who took care of water and safety inspections. The Drinking Water Surveillance Program, which closely monitored the quality of water across the province, had been eliminated by the government in 1997. The Environmental Approvals Improvement Act was passed that same year. It explicitly prohibited "legal action against the government by anyone adversely affected by the Environment Minister's failure to apply environmental regulations."

Government legislation also failed to deal with the increasing size of farms. Sanitation laws seemed relevant to small family farms, but the laws didn't address the effects on the environment that were possible from factory farming. It is estimated that 1200 pigs—not an unusual number on factory farms—can produce as much waste as 60,000 humans. Therefore, a single farm can require the same scale of sewage treatment as would a mid-sized city.

For his part, Harris blamed the previous NDP provincial government who had loosened regulations for utilities. Ultimately, the Conservative government was defeated in the next election, partly because of the unpopularity of their handling of the Walkerton Tragedy.

Air France Flight 358 Crash

A TERRIBLE DISASTER—but one that could have been much worse—occurred on August 2, 2005, when an Air France jet attempted a scheduled landing at Toronto Pearson International Airport.

The plane had taken off from Paris that morning and went through an uneventful trip across the Atlantic. However, when the pilot attempted to land the plane in Toronto at 8:01 PM, it was unable to stop and plunged off the end of the runway into a ravine. The accident may have been due to the stormy conditions, which included heavy rain and high winds. Some of the passengers reported feeling the plane rock dangerously from side to side before touching down. In any case, it seems that the storm blocked the pilot's view, and he landed the plane too far down the runway, in a position that didn't give it enough room to stop on the slippery pavement. Later inspections showed that the brakes had been working.

The jet came to a stop 200 metres past the runway and quickly burst into flames. Miraculously, all 297 passengers and 12 crew members were evacuated before the plane exploded and burned completely. Of the 309 people on board, 43 suffered injuries, but none of them serious.

Some of the passengers and crew, dazed from the crash, stumbled out onto the nearby 401 Expressway, where they flagged down vehicles. The motorists who stopped drove a few people, including the pilot, directly to hospital.

Wreckage from an Air France plane that overshot the runway at Toronto Pearson International Airport in 2005. Luckily, all passengers and crew survived.

~⚭~

Although the fire had blocked some of the emergency exits on the plane, rescue crews along with the plane's crew managed to complete the evacuation in less than two minutes. The rescue operation was hailed in the press as a model process.

Immediately after the crash, Air France offered cash payments to the survivors, as well as free trips to anywhere in the world. However, there is now a class action lawsuit against the airline that is still waiting to go to court.

Kashechewan *E. Coli* Outbreak

THE REMOTE NORTHERN ONTARIO Cree community of Kashechewan was evacuated, beginning on October 26, 2005. It took nine days to move the 1900 residents to temporary housing in Cochrane, Timmins and Sudbury.

The reason for the evacuation was a devastating outbreak of *E. coli* bacteria, which stemmed from a flood that had occurred in the town. It was the same type of bacteria that had led to the Walkerton tragedy in southern Ontario five years earlier.

However, unlike Walkerton, in which the poisonings were stopped through an advisory to boil all water and the ordering of shipments of bottled water, Kashechewan had to totally evacuate. It was clear from the outset that years of government neglect and a bias in favour of the heavily populated area south of the province had allowed the housing and water system of the town to slip to Third World levels.

The constant flooding that Kashechewan experienced had led to calls by concerned citizens to move the town, which they thought was unsanitary and dangerous. Sites near Fort Albany and Timmins were both considered as alternative sites, but no action was taken. In fact, Kashechewan had originally been part of Fort Albany. It was founded in the 1950s, after the original Hudson Bay settlement of Fort Albany was divided in two, along Anglican-Catholic religious lines. One half kept its original name, but the two technically remained part of the same reserve.

In Kashechewan, residents had been boiling their drinking water for 10 years prior. The town, where it was normal for as many as 17 people to share a single, flimsy house, had limited electricity and virtually no water purification system. What system there was failed to separate drinking water from sewage and had to use dangerous levels of chemicals. Boiling the large amounts of water required for a bath was difficult, and the only means of doing so were wood-burning stoves. In addition, the surrounding area had been stripped of trees as the community struggled to keep warm and clean.

E. coli was first discovered in Kashechewan on October 14, following a flood. A raw sewage lagoon was dangerously close to the swollen Red Willow Creek, where the community got its water.

Although most of the bacteria had disappeared by October 17, it was still necessary to flush out the town's water system with chlorine. When residents of Kashechewan drank the only safe water available—which was highly chlorinated—they found it unpleasant, and the chemicals actually caused pre-existing skin conditions to worsen. The residents, it was discovered, had been subjected to irregular levels of chlorine. When the chlorine injector broke down in the water system, local workers just roughly estimated the amount needed and added it manually. It was later revealed that the chlorine injector— a $30 piece—was dangerously dirty and may have itself been causing contamination.

The immediate effects of the poisoning included a weakening of the townspeople's immune system, especially among young children. Residents did not drink the tap water, but they did shower and bathe in it. Scabies, impetigo and eczema all became widespread.

"There were a lot of problems with the kids," Chief Leo Friday told the *Toronto Star*. "If they had a wound, a sore, it would not heal."

Although no was killed directly by the outbreak, scores became seriously ill.

The father of a boy reportedly begged for airfare to send his son to Timmins. The sores had disfigured his face so much that other children at school were making fun of him.

"My grandchildren have rashes all over and they scratch them raw in the night and there is blood all over," town resident Annabelle Wesley told *The Star*. "It's been almost two weeks ago. We need clean water so we can shower again."

Eventually, the whole town was evacuated. But when they returned on December 28, they found their homes in bad shape. The advisory to boil water continued to be in effect. Cold weather had cracked the pipes in many houses, and the flood had caused serious damage, including toxic mould. The local school was condemned because the mould situation had become so bad.

A report by the Ministry of the Environment stated that Kashechewan would need to completely overhaul its water system. It would require government inspections—which had never occurred before—separate water and sewage pipes, changes to the chemicals that were used and trained workers.

"Nobody really trained us," admitted water treatment worker Alfred Wesley to the *Toronto Star*. He also conceded that the alarm system in the treatment building had been disabled. "It used to make a lot of noise, going off all the time. We just shut it off."

Many in the community urged that blame not be placed on the operators, since they lacked even rudimentary training.

"I call those guys Einstein," band executive member Archie Wesley told *The Star*. "Without training, without tools, without a proper water treatment plant, they've managed not to kill anybody in this community."

The government argued that an engineer's report—which urged Kashechewan's band leaders to eliminate beaver dams on Red Willow Creek and follow a three-year maintenance plan—had been ignored. The band argued that it had never been shown the report and that it did not have enough funding for proper maintenance.

Most people in southern Ontario had never heard of Kashechewan, let alone the massive problems that the community faced. However, a series of front-page articles in the *Toronto Star* and the *Globe and Mail* brought the crisis to a wider audience. It soon came out that as many as 14 other Aboriginal communities in northern Ontario faced similar problems. Because water systems on reserves falls under federal, rather than provincial, jurisdiction, they were subject to much less scrutiny. The disaster in Kashechewan could have happened in any of these communities.

"We have no ideas what viruses might be in the polluted water, we need hepatitis A and B vaccine free for everyone in this community," said Dr. Murray Trussler, chief of staff at the Weeneebayko General Hospital in Moose Factory. Trussler was also shocked to hear that a water treatment plant could be located downstream from a sewage lagoon.

"[Whoever built the plant] obviously didn't know much about public health, and it's a disgrace," he said.

Federal funding for reserve water systems was based on the number of families living in each one. However, it assumed an average family size of four. In Kashechewan, families often exceeded 10 people. Kashechewan also had to share its funding equally with the smaller Fort Albany, even though the two communities were far apart and should have had two separate water systems.

A report by the Ontario First Nations Technical Services Corporation showed that 95 out of 134 reserves in Ontario had medium to high risks of an *E. coli* outbreak.

"I'm not saying I am glad to see *E. coli*, but what does it take for the government to see what the native people are going through here and across Canada?" asked Rebecca Friday of Kashechewan to *The Star*.

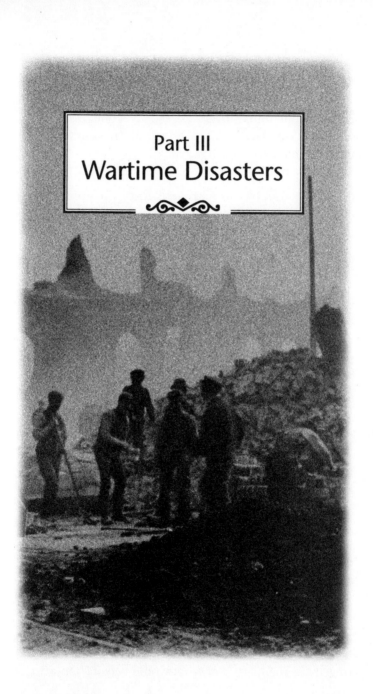

Part III
Wartime Disasters

Wendat Genocide

1600–1650
Huronia (Simcoe County)

Many European North Americans today imagine that the continent they live on was mostly uninhabited before their ancestors' arrival. However, historians disagree. No reliable figures are available for the Americas' population in the year 1500, but estimates are that it was over 100 million. That would put it on par with Europe's population at the time. Estimates of Ontario's original population go as high as 200,000.

Many Aboriginal people died as a result of diseases that they had not developed immunities to. Others died because of collapses in their economies that occurred during that period, while others were outright killed by Europeans or rival North American nations.

Some historians use the word "genocide" to describe the deaths that occurred across the continent, whereas others consider the word inappropriate. The debate centres around the degree to which early European settlers intended to wipe out existing Aboriginal nations.

All of this aside, there is no doubt that the sudden collapse of Wendat—once the most powerful trading nation in Ontario—can be considered a genocide. Between 1600 and 1650, the Wendat population dropped from over 30,000 to less than 1600.

The elimination of the Wendat happened through a combination of disease, political bad luck and scheming by their enemies. It remains perhaps the greatest human tragedy in the history of what would become Ontario.

The Wendat were actually a confederation of five nations—the Arendarhonon, Attigneenongnahac, the Attignawantan, the Tahontaenrat and the Ataronchronon. Today, little is known that would distinguish the groups from each other. The people were famous for their agriculture, having cleared the forests around Lake Simcoe and Lake Huron to make way for massive cornfields. Fishing and rice cultivation were their other means of sustenance.

But most importantly, the Wendat managed to occupy a key piece of real estate. Their central location made them brokers of trade between the Haudenosaunee (or Six Nations Confederacy) and Neutrals to the south, and the Cree and Ojibway to the north. They controlled the key "Toronto" trading route between Lake Simcoe and Lake Ontario.

(The French named the Wendat "Hurons," after a slang word for "a big clump of hair." Ironically, the hairstyle is now associated with one of the enemies of the Wendat, the Mohawks. Lake Huron is named after the Wendat, and their traditional homeland around Lake Simcoe is still known as Huronia. In this book, however, the word "Wendat" will be used, which is more accurate.)

Soon after the establishment of New France, the French sought out the Wendat people for a partnership. A formal alliance was formed in 1611, which pitted the French and Wendat against the English and their Aboriginal allies, the Haudenosaunee. Indeed, the Wendat had been fighting the Seneca, one of the component nations of the Haudenosaunee, since at least 1609. The source of the conflict is thought to have been over access to European trading goods.

The first French colony in Ontario, a religious mission known as Ste. Marie, was established deep in Huronia in 1639. By this point, many of the Wendat had already died of diseases, which hit hardest in the 1630s. Thousands died of smallpox and the plague. A number converted to Christianity, but the conversions weakened the traditional order of Wendat society. Christians and non-Christians refused to cooperate in day-to-day life. The economy began to weaken, as did the military situation for the Wendat.

The French had been reluctant to trade guns to the Wendat—only in 1641 did they start giving firearms to the most trusted of converts. However, the English and Dutch were more than happy to arm the Wendat's rivals, the Haudenosaunee, with a large supply.

By 1648, the way of life for the Wendat deteriorated. The Haudenosaunee launched greater and greater attacks on Wendat towns, eventually breaking and then razing their fortifications. Cornfields were burned, and many people were systematically killed or captured. With the loss of their major towns and cornfields, many Wendat either starved or froze. And France did not have enough of its own soldiers in North America to effectively intervene. In the chaos of the Wendat-Haudenosaunee conflict, a number of French missionaries were captured, tortured and killed.

In 1649, the French decided they could no longer hold Ste. Marie, and they abandoned it. The surviving missionaries retreated to Québec City, taking with them several hundred Wendat converts, who had desperately sought refuge on Christian Island. These people, who call themselves "Huron-Wendats," still live at Wendake, near Québec City. The last speaker of the Wendat language died there in the late 19th century.

The surviving non-Christian Wendat made a peace agreement with the Haudenosaunee and fled to Ohio and Michigan. They lived successfully there for some time, but due to a series of unsuccessful alliances, wound up being pushed farther southwest to Kansas and Oklahoma.

Many of the captured Wendat became assimilated into the Haudenosaunee nations. By the second generation, they were even allowed to assume leadership positions there. The famous Mohawk chief Joseph Brant is often described as being of partial or full Wendat heritage.

With the elimination of the Wendat, the Haudenosaunee attempted to colonize southern Ontario and monopolize trade with the northern Ontario nations. However, they faced a number of setbacks, and Ojibway and English settlers eventually seized control of much of the area.

Scattered across the continent, the Wendat population is today estimated at 8000. In 1999, representatives of the surviving Wendat groups reconvened in their traditional homeland and declared the Wendat confederacy reestablished. They have recently been involved in a struggle to preserve a traditional burial ground in Vaughan, Ontario, from being built over.

Fort York Explosion
and Burning of York

$\sim$❖$\sim$

April 27–May 2, 1813
York (Toronto)

ONE OF THE GREATEST TRAGEDIES of the War of 1812 was the near-total destruction of Upper Canada's capital city—not that York was much of a city at the time.

In 1813, York had a mere 600 citizens. It stretched only 10 small square blocks, between Palace (now Front) Street and Duchess (now Richmond) Street, and between George and Ontario streets. It was the capital of Upper Canada but had no mayor of municipal government (it would not have one until 1834, when it was renamed "Toronto"). The town's defences had not been completed yet, there was little artillery, and the tiny fort, some ways outside of York, could do little to protect it.

In 1813, the Americans were looking for an invasion target in Upper Canada. They hoped to make military gains and to further their propaganda campaign. The war's aims were always unclear, and public opinion, especially in large East Coast American cities, was turning against the conflict and President James Madison, who had initiated it.

At the time, Kingston was the main military stronghold in Upper Canada, with its Martello Towers and the massive stone battements of Fort Henry. American intelligence discovered that Kingston was being guarded by 8000 soldiers, though in fact only about 600 were there.

Because Kingston seemed too intimidating, the Americans chose York as a symbolic target. An amphibious invading force of about 1800 Americans set out from Sacketts Harbor, New York, under the command of Brigadier General Zebulon Pike.

York was defended by a mere 300 soldiers under the leadership of Major General Roger Hale Sheaffe, plus 100 Mississauga and Ojibway allies. It was clear from the outset that they had no chance of keeping the Americans at bay, especially since they had no idea where their enemy might land.

The Americans decided to come ashore near the mouth of the Humber River and to march east towards York. After a few skirmishes, Sheaffe ordered his soldiers to abandon the city and told local militia leaders to negotiate a surrender. However, he secretly also ordered that the incomplete battleship *Isaac Brock* being built in the harbour be burned. The ship would have been the largest warship in the Great Lakes, and Sheaffe feared that the Americans might capture it and complete it for themselves.

More controversially, it was alleged that Sheaffe booby-trapped Fort York as he left, though this has never been proven. In any case, the moment the American army entered the fort, a gunpowder storage house exploded. The explosion shattered the stone buildings, raining rocks over both the charging Americans and fleeing British.

In all, 38 Americans were killed and another 222 were wounded. On the British side, 62 were killed and 77 wounded. Five members of the militia were killed and another five wounded, while eight of the Aboriginal allies were killed.

British Lieutenant Ely Playter, who had returned to the fort to get his coat, described himself being "in a horrid situation, the stones falling thick as hail and large ones sinking into the very earth."

The most notable casualty was Brigadier General Pike himself, who was crushed by a large boulder thrown into the air by the explosion.

The Americans were bitter about what they considered a cowardly trick on the part of Sheaffe, and the surrender took a long time to negotiate. Meanwhile, American soldiers plundered and burned the town of York, terrorizing the civilian population. Nearly every public building was burned, including the town blockhouse, the Government House, the jail, the docks, the fort, its barracks and some public warehouses. A number of private houses were also burned, and several civilians were killed.

On May 1, the wooden Parliament buildings were burned to the ground. Most historical records blame American sailors for the destruction of Upper Canada's first purpose-built Parliament buildings, though others suggest that it was done by Canadian fugitives set free during the burning of the jail.

Finally, on May 2, the Americans left, taking with them a small, older warship from the harbour, as well as a number of small cannons.

The messiness of the whole invasion, including the explosion and arson, caused outrage on both sides of the border. Residents of York were angered that the town had not been properly defended. Sheaffe found himself demoted and recalled to Britain.

The occupation of York cut off British supply and communication lines to Lake Erie, later leading to the defeat of the British fleet. Allegedly in retribution for the burning of York, the British army burned Washington, DC, and besieged Baltimore. These attacks increased popular opposition to the war in the United States, and eventually led to a peace treaty. In the end—despite horrendous bloodshed—the War of 1812 was a stalemate.

It would take years to undo the damage done to York, but the city continued to grow and prosper. Plans were soon underway for new brick Parliament buildings. A larger fort was built at York, but the town would never become a major military garrison.

Notes on Sources

Cholera Outbreaks
Bilson, Geoffrey. *A Darkened House*. Toronto: University of Toronto Press, 1980.
Komoka Train Wreck
The Globe and Mail, March 2, 1874. Front Page.
Spanish Influenza
Pettigrew, Eileen. *Silent Enemy*. Saskatoon: Western Producer Prairie Books, 1983.
PBS: http://www.pbs.org/wgbh/amex/influenza/sfeature/drjef-frey12.htm
Heat Wave of 1936
The Globe and Mail, July 10 and 11, 1936.
The Weather Doctor: http://www.islandnet.com/~see/weather/almanac/arc2006/alm06jul.htm
http://www.citizenreviewonline.org/July_2006/18/heatwave.html
Thames River Flood
The Globe and Mail, April 27 and 28, 1937.
http://www.thamesriver.on.ca/Water_Management/flood_history.htm
Windsor Tornado
The Globe and Mail, June 18 and 19, 1946.
Winisk River Flood
"Flooding Events in Canada – Ontario." http://www.ec.gc.ca/water/en/manage/floodgen/e_ont.htm
http://www.ourvoices.ca/index/winisk
The Globe and Mail, May 19 and 20, 1986.
Kirkland Lake Mine Collapse
The Globe and Mail, November 27, 29–30, 1993; December 1, 4, 30, 1993; February 11, 1994.
SARS Epidemic
The Toronto Star, October 19, 2003.
"Ethics and SARS: Learning Lessons from the Toronto Experience." University of Toronto Joint Centre for Bioethics: http://www.yorku.ca/igreene/sars.html
http://www.jerryamernic.com/video.shtml
Sinking of the *Commerce*
The Globe and Mail, May 9, 1850.
Baptiste Creek Train Collision
The Globe and Mail, October 31, 1854.

London City Hall Collapse
Doty, Christopher. "Dead Weight." London History. http://www.
dotydocs.com/Archives/disasters/city%20hall.htm
The Globe and Mail, January 4 and 5, 1898.
Ottawa-Hull Fire
St. John, Edward S. Bytown Pamphlet Series #1-14. Ottawa:
Historical Society of Ottawa, 1983.
Munitions Plant Explosion
The Globe and Mail, October 14, 1918.
Trans-Canada Airlines Crash
The Globe and Mail, February 7, 11, 12 and March 6, 1941.
American Airlines DC-3 Crash
Winchester, Dawson. "63rd Anniversary of Tragic Elgin Air
Disaster." St. Thomas Times-Journal, October 30, 2004.
http://cgi.bowesonline.com/pedro.php?id=5&x=story&xid=124
423
The Globe and Mail, November 1, 1941. p. 13.
Sinking of the *Wawinet*
The Globe and Mail, September 23, 1942, pp. 1–2.
Coniston Bus-Train Crash
The Globe and Mail, February 10 and 12, 1951.
Williamsburg Canal Bus Crash
The Globe and Mail, August 1, 1953.
RCAF Crash into Convent
The Globe and Mail, May 16, 17, 1956.
http://www.scohs.on.ca/bins/news_display_page.asp?cid=11-
113-3303&lang=1
Gas Explosion at Metropolitan Store
The Globe and Mail, October 26, 1960, pp. 11 and 17.
Air Canada Flight 621 Crash
The Globe and Mail, July 6, 1970.
Barrie Highway Collision
The Globe and Mail, March 19, 1973.
Bus-Train Crash
The Globe and Mail, December 12 and 15, 1975.
http://www.biggeworld.com/archive/npambulance.html
Air Canada Flight 189 Crash
The Globe and Mail, June 27, 1978.
Nursing Home Fire
The Globe and Mail, July 15 and 16, 1980.
Air Ontario Flight 1363 Crash
The Globe and Mail, pp. 1 and 2, March 11 and 13, 1989.
Cobalt Highway Crash
The Globe and Mail, July 30, 1991.
Toronto Subway Crash
"At least two die in Toronto subway crash." *The Globe and Mail,*
August 12, 1995, p. A1.

Kashechewan *E. Coli* Outbreak

"Reserve water crisis sparks major changes for aboriginals." *The Edmonton Journal,* December 28, 2005.

The Sudbury Star, November 28 and December 19, 2005.

Canadian Press Newswire, December 6, 2005.

The Globe and Mail, November 11, 2005.

The Toronto Star, October 27, November 4 and 12, 2005.

General Sources

"The 200 Year History of the St. Lawrence Market – Part One." http://www.travelandtransitions.com/stories_photos/to_stories_stlawrence1.htm

Abley, Mark, ed. *Stories from the Ice Storm.* Toronto: McClelland & Stewart Inc., 1999.

"About the St. Lawrence Hall." http://www.cestwhat.com/news.asp

Barcus, Frank. *Freshwater Fury: Yarns and Reminiscences of the Greatest Storm in Inland Navigation.* Detroit: Wayne State University Press, 1960. (Good map of all the Great Lakes and locations of ship disasters on inside cover.)

Benn, Carl. *Battle of York.* Belleville: Mika Publishing Company, 1984.

Bourrie, Mark. *Many a Midnight Ship.* Toronto: Key Porter Books, 2005.

Bourrie, Mark. *Ninety Fathoms Down.* Toronto: Hounslow Press, 1995.

Bourrie, Mark. "Anxiety, mourning for lost trees legacy of Barrie tornado children." *The Globe and Mail.* August 9, 1986. p. A11.

Bowen, Dana Thomas. *Shipwrecks of the Great Lakes.* Cleveland: Freshwater Press Inc., 1952.

Boyer, Dwight. *Ghost Ships of the Great Lakes.* Toronto: McClelland and Stewart Ltd., 1968.

City of Mississauga: http://www.mississauga.ca/portal/residents/localhistory?paf_gear_id=9700018&itemId=5500001

Cochrane, Hugh. *Gateway to Oblivion: The Great Lakes' Bermuda Triangle.* Toronto: Doubleday Canada Ltd., 1980.

Diemer, Ulli. "Contamination: The Poisonous Legacy of Ontario's Environmental Cutbacks." http://www.diemer.ca/Docs/Diemer-Contamination.htm

European Disease Epidemics in Native Americans; Huron History: http://www.kporterfield.com/aicttw/articles/disease.html

Gifford, Jim. *Hurricane Hazel.* Toronto: Dundurn Press, 2004.

Graham, Paul. *DISASTER! Canadian Catastrophes.* Toronto: Canadian Reinsurance Company, 1992.

Gray, John. "The Fire that Wiped Out Porcupine." In: *In the Face of Disaster: True Stories of Canadian Heroism from the Archives of Maclean's.* Toronto: Penguin Books Canada Ltd., 2000.

Great Lakes Shipwreck Files: http://www.boatnerd.com/
swayze/shipwreck/o.htm

Halliday, Hugh A. *Wreck!: Canada's Worst Railway Accidents.*
Toronto: Robin Brass Studio. 1997.

Hemming, Robert J. *Ships Gone Missing.* Chicago: Contemporary
Books, 1992.

Jackson, Jonathan. "Tragedy on the Lakes: The Great Storm
of 1913's 'Unprecedented Violence' Claimed Some 250 Lives."
Maclean's. Toronto. October 27, 2003, Vol. 116, Iss. 43, p. 45.

"Joseph S. Fay: One of Many 1905 Storm Victims." http://per-
durabo10.tripod.com/ships/id24.html

"The Kam Kotia Mine Disaster: Ontario's Most Notorious Mine
Waste Problem." http://www.miningwatch.ca/index.php?/
AMD/Kam_Kotia_Highgrader

Looker, Janet. *Disaster Canada.* Toronto: Lynx Images, 2000.

MacInnis, Dr. Joseph. *Fitzgerald's Storm.* Toronto: MacMillan
Canada, 1997.

Maritime History of the Great Lakes: http://www.hhpl.on.ca/
GreatLakes/Wrecks/

"The Protection of Bridges." http://www.catskillarchive.com/
rrextra/wkbkch12.Html

"Rehabilitation of Kam Kotia Mine." http://www.mndm.gov.
on.ca/mndm/mines/mg/abanmin/kamkotia_e.asp

Rogers, Edward S., and Donald B. Smith. *Aboriginal Ontario:
Historical Perspectives on the First Nations.* Toronto: Dundurn Press
Ltd., 1994.

Ryerson, Stanley. B. *The Founding of Canada: Beginnings to 1815.*
Toronto: Progress Books, 1975.

Shkilnyk, Anastasia. *A Poison Stronger Than Love: The Destruction of
an Ojibwa Community.* Westford, Massachusetts: Yale University,
1985.

Simon, Laurent, and Thierry C. Pauchant. *Developing the
Three Levels of Learning in Crisis Management: A Case Study of the
Hagersville Tire Fire.* Review of Business, 2000.

"Springbank Park." http://cec.chebucto.org/ClosPark/Sp-Bank.html

Stacy, Colonel C.P. *The Battle of Little York.* Toronto: Toronto
Historical Board, 1963.

Varkaris, Jane, and Lucile Finsten. *Fire on Parliament Hill!* Erin,
ON: The Boston Mills Press, 1988.

http://archives.cbc.ca

http://en.wikipedia.org/wiki/Wikipedia:Contents

http://www.ainc-inac.gc.ca/ch/rcap/sg/si20_e.html

http://www.allmusic.com

http://www.boatnerd.com

http://www.history.ca/

http://www.michiganshipwrecks.org/armistice.htm

http://www.poliocanada.com/english/barbara_bondar.asp

http://www.thecanadianencyclopedia.com

René Biberstein

RENÉ BIBERSTEIN WAS BORN IN TORONTO and spent part of his childhood in Switzerland. He studied journalism at Concordia University, won the Concordia Media Award and was voted the best journalist on campus by his fellow students. He went on to freelance for Toronto's *Now* magazine, the *Montreal Mirror, Tart,* and the Globe and Mail Online Edition. René also spent two years as a walking tour guide in southern Ontario. He is fascinated by the way places affect people's lives and plans to study urban planning at Ryerson University. René has published two other non-fiction books.